Rattling, Calling & Decoying Whitetails

How to Consistently Coax Big Bucks into Range

by
Gary Clancy

Edited by Patrick Durkin

Published by

krause
publications

700 E. State St. • Iola, WI 54990-0001
Telephone: 715/445-2214
fax: 715/445-4087
World Wide Web:
www.deeranddeerhunting.com

Please call or write for our free catalog of outdoor publications.
Our toll-free number to place an order or obtain a free catalog is
800-258-0929. Please use our regular business telephone
715-445-2214 for editorial comment or further information.

Library of Congress Catalog Number: 99-67145
ISBN: 0-87341-833-6
Printed in the United States of America

Cover photo by Mike Searles

Photography by Gary Clancy, Ian McMurchy

Illustrated maps by Dave Beauchaine

Deer & Deer Hunting is a registered trademark of Krause Publications Inc.

Dedication

*To my wife, Nancy Clancy, for understanding,
even though you do not share my passion
for the whitetail.
Thanks for keeping the home fires
burning when I'm out hunting bucks
like the one pictured here!*

Contents

Acknowledgments

I plead guilty to being a whitetail addict. White-tailed deer have interested me for as long as I can remember, long before I ever hunted them. And even though my passion now is hunting mature bucks, I never tire of watching any whitetail, be it a doe, fawn or young buck.

When I got the idea to write this book, it was not so much that I wanted to write another book in order to support my family. I've written or co-written three books before this one, and I know from experience that the effort that goes into making a good book would be more rewarding financially if it were channeled into another endeavor. But this book is special to me. Nothing is more exciting than calling or rattling in a white-tailed buck, unless, of course, you put a decoy into the picture. The bottom line is that these three tactics are a barrel of fun, and I wanted other deer hunters and future deer hunters to share that enjoyment. This book is my attempt to do that.

Although it would have been easier, I did not sit in my recliner and dream up all of the information in this book. Nor did I spend days glued to my computer's monitor "surfing the net" to glean the nuggets you'll find in these pages. The deer woods are my research library. There may be some hunters who spend more time than I do in the places whitetails call home, but darned few.

And even though I probably could have written a book based solely on my own experiences with calling, rattling and decoying deer, it would have been more of an ego trip than an honest attempt to give you the information that makes these tactics work. That is why I picked the brains of some of the best deer hunters I know. I wanted to share the lessons these hard-core whitetail nuts have learned and shared with me. The list is too long and I'm afraid I would forget to mention somebody, but you know who you are and I thank you.

I would also like to thank Patrick Durkin, the editor of *Deer & Deer Hunting* magazine, who made time from his busy schedule to edit this book. As an editor who also happens to be a pretty fair whitetail hunter, Durkin transforms even my scribbling into entertaining and educating prose.

Introduction

I had just finished giving a seminar on calling, rattling and decoying at the annual Deer Classic in Madison, Wis. This event attracts between 15,000 and 20,000 rabid whitetail fans each year.

After my seminar, a group of hunters gathered around me to ask more specific questions. As we talked, I noticed an elderly man sitting patiently in the second row of seats. I assumed he was waiting for one of the younger hunters, perhaps a grandson, to finish picking what was left of my brain.

But I was wrong. The old hunter waited until everyone left, and then slowly made his way over. "I liked your little talk," he began. "Lots of nice pictures, too. But let me ask you something. I'm 79 years old; be 80 by next deer season. I still go deer hunting every year. Don't walk as far as I used to, but that's all right, because I get to post on every drive.

"Now, Jake, that's my oldest boy, he just retired from the Post Office. He's been writing everything down since he was a little feller, so for the last 45 years we have a pretty good record of our hunts. Only been seven times in those 45 years I didn't get a deer, so what the hell do I need with a grunt call, rattling horns and a decoy?"

"That's a remarkable record, sir," I answered. "If I were you, I would just go right on doing what you've been doing."

"That's what I figured," the old man said, now obviously pleased. We shook hands and the old hunter walked away.

Like that old hunter, not everyone will benefit from calling, rattling or decoying. But if I've learned one thing from my years of talking to hunters, many of them aren't satisfied to hunt the same way year after year. Maybe that's because they aren't as successful as that old man.

Then again, I can't promise this book will make you any more successful than you are now. But I've tried my hardest to help. It took me years of hunting and comparing notes with top deer hunters to compile this book. Furthermore, this is my first chance to put everything I've learned on rattling, calling and decoying into one, tightly wrapped package.

No matter what your reason for picking up this book, and no matter how long you've been hunting whitetails, I hope you'll find my advice helpful. After all, now that I've put everything I know about these topics under one cover, my brain has been picked dry. I guess that means if I'm going to teach you anything, it's now or never. There's no turning back. Good luck.

— *Gary Clancy*
December 1999

CHAPTER 1

Why Bother Trying This Stuff?

The opening of the firearms deer season in Wisconsin is a big deal, perhaps even surpassing the annual matchups between the Green Bay Packers and Minnesota Vikings. Some schools and businesses still shut their doors for the entire nine-day hunt because teachers, students and workers have all gone hunting anyway.

As a result, nearly 750,000 hunters hit the woods the Saturday before Thanksgiving each year. And, as the wry observer often notes, those who aren't deer hunting are either married to a hunter or wishing they were.

All those hunters, however, produce a few problems. For instance, unless you have exclusive access to a large chunk of private property, calling and rattling are usually a waste of effort under such intense hunting pressure. Furthermore, dragging out and setting up a decoy could be suicidal during such an invasion of hunters.

Ask yourself these questions when pondering if it's worth calling, rattling or using a decoy: Will the deer be moving because of the rut's influences or because they're on their way to feeding or bedding areas? Or, on the other hand, are the deer moving because of hunting pressure? If natural movement explains deer activity, you might want to consider calling, rattling and decoying tactics. But if the deer are moving because of hunting pressure, the tactics we'll discuss in this book will waste your time and might even be detrimental to your hunt.

Therefore, from here on out, I'm assuming you're hunting deer that are relatively undisturbed by hunting pressure. But let me clarify one thing: I'm not saying these techniques won't work during the general firearms season. White-tailed deer, especially those in rut, can quickly react to a decrease in hunting pressure and return to their routines once most hunters have gone home. I've had some great success calling and rattling at midweek during the gun season.

Reasons to Try

I can think of many excellent reasons to consider rattling, calling and decoying deer. Let's look at calling first. Calling can be used to attract deer that you otherwise might never have seen. I call this technique "calling blind." Calls can also be used to entice deer that are in sight but out of

Although I've occasionally rattled in bucks I could see, rattling is usually an act of faith. You must believe there is a buck out there within earshot of your rattling horns, and that he will dance to horn music.

When a buck comes into a decoy, no matter if it responded to calling, rattling, a combination of the two, or neither, its focus is on the decoy.

range to come closer. This is a big advantage, especially for bow-hunters. Calling can also calm deer that otherwise might have spooked. In addition, it's a great way to start off a rattling sequence, which we'll look at next.

I compare rattling and calling to my phone bill. Using a call is the local part of my bill. Rattling is my long-distance service, the AT&T route. On a quiet, cool morning you can really reach out and touch 'em with a set of rattling horns. Rattling can allow you to see bucks (and does) that you otherwise wouldn't have known existed. Although I've occasionally rattled in bucks I could see, rattling is usually an act of faith. You must believe there is a buck out there within earshot of your rattling horns, and that he will dance to horn music.

And then there is decoying. In most cases, a decoy provides the visual confirmation a buck seeks when responding to a call or rattling horns. He heard a deer, and now he wants to see a deer. Far fewer deer that respond to a call or rattling horns will hang up out of range if you have a decoy in place to close the deal. But even though most deer approaching a decoy were first enticed with calling or rattling, that's not a case-hardened rule. I've had many deer respond to my decoys on their own. In these cases, they were just passing by when they spotted the decoy and came over to check out the new guy (or gal) in town.

When a buck comes into a decoy, no matter if it responded to calling, rattling, a combination of the two, or neither, its focus is on the decoy. For bow-hunters, especially, this behavior creates a huge advantage. Unless you dance a heavy-footed polka on your tree stand while a buck approaches the decoy, he won't spot you. Naturally, this also makes it far easier to draw the bow undetected. A properly positioned decoy also helps provide a broadside or quartering-away shot at any buck that approaches the decoy. And if you like to videotape your hunt, as many hunters are doing these days, a decoy makes it easier to position the camera and film the deer. This will provide you with some of your most treasured footage.

The Fun Factor

All of those considerations are practical, legitimate reasons for including calling, rattling and decoying in your bag of tricks. Even so, I can think of

In most cases, a decoy provides the visual confirmation a buck seeks when responding to a call or rattling horns.

High hunter pressure can be detrimental to the effects of rattling, calling and decoying. Natural deer movement is preferred when using these tactics.

a better reason to try these tactics: They're exciting! Some hunters seem to forget that deer hunting is supposed to be fun. If all of the emphasis is on filling your tag, getting the camp's biggest buck, or putting one in "the book," it's difficult to relax and have fun during the hunt. When the kill, not the hunt, becomes a hunter's focus, fun can't enter the picture. Suddenly, deer hunting becomes serious business.

Sure, these tactics work for those who choose to make killing a deer their top priority, but you're missing a lot when you intentionally concentrate on results. Believe me, I've been there, so I know.

Have fun with calling, rattling and decoying. You'll see more deer if you use any or all of these tactics, and for most hunters, seeing deer is a big part of the enjoyment of deer hunting. Chances are good you'll see deer do things you've never seen before. Deer coming to a call, horns or decoy often put on a show. In fact, some of the deer antics I've seen when they interact with a decoy made me laugh out loud in my tree stand.

Enough said. Let's go learn how to have fun!

CHAPTER 2

The Whitetail's Vocalizations

S ilent ghosts of the forest. Chances are, I read that description of the white-tailed deer in one of the outdoor magazines I consumed during my misdirected youth. That characterization of whitetails seemed to fit. After all, the only sound I had ever heard from a deer was the "blowing" or "snorting" that let every deer in the county know about me.

In fact, if I had brought up deer vocalizations at the campfire back in the late 1950s, or even the '60s and '70s, I would have drawn big laughs from the boys. Although outdoor writers were beginning to discuss calling and deer vocalizations in the early 1980s, and a couple of manufacturers were making deer calls, it really wasn't until the late 1980s and early 1990s that deer calling became popular with the hunting masses.

Today, we know whitetails are far more vocal than anyone believed a few years ago. But learning the extent of their vocalizations wasn't really that shocking of a revelation. In fact, it all makes sense when we consider the supporting facts. For example, deer are social critters. Does and fawns live in family groups. Bucks, although solitary much of the year, hang out in bachelor groups in summer through early autumn. And in the North Woods, deer commonly yard for the winter in sizable herds. Animals in a group need to communicate, and deer do that with a variety of sounds.

Researchers studying whitetail vocalizations differ somewhat when categorizing the whitetail's vocalizations. The most famous study — conducted at the University of Georgia in 1988 by Larry Marchinton, Karl Miller and Tom Atkinson — identified 90 different sounds that they grouped into 12 vocalizations most often used by whitetails. These sounds are the maternal grunt, nursing whine, mew, bleat, tending grunt, contact grunt, Flehmen sniff, grunt-snort-wheeze, grunt-snort, snort, bawl and low grunt.

To keep it simple, I break the 12 into just three sounds: the grunt, the snort and the bleat. Each of these three basic vocalizations has several variations, and each means something different in the whitetail's world.

Speak the Language

Calling deer is not difficult, but it pays to know what a specific sound

White-tailed deer are not the mute, silent creatures we often picture. Fawns and does, for example, communicate in often hard-to-hear mews and bleats.

There's no need to describe every vocalization made by whitetails, because many sounds deer make are so quiet that they must be within bow range to hear it.

means before you use it, otherwise you could say the wrong thing at the wrong time. Gary Sefton, one of North America's most knowledgeable callers, is fond of saying, "The trick to calling anything is knowing what to say, when to say it, and what the call should sound like."

I can't say it any better.

Because this book is for hunters, there's no need to describe every vocalization made by whitetails, because many sounds deer make are so quiet that they must be within bow range to hear it.

Not only that, but it would be difficult for most hunters to reproduce these obscure vocalizations because not one manufacturer makes such calls. I find this all interesting, however. I've spent a lifetime in close contact with whitetails, and I would have bet I had heard all of their vocalizations at some point. That's a bet I would have lost. Even if I had been within bow range, I probably would not have heard them.

I know this from firsthand experience. Let me explain. A couple of years ago, I tried out the Walker Game Ear device, albeit somewhat reluctantly because I have great hearing. I figured I could not possibly gain anything by wearing the device.

But on my first early-season bow-hunt of the year, I slipped in the Game Ear. (Hey, I wasn't going to wait for the rut and then find out the thing actually hampered my hearing!) That first evening I had a doe and twin fawns around my stand for about 10 minutes and, because of the Game Ear, I heard the fawns making incredibly soft mews as a way to stay in touch with the doe. The doe responded with equally soft bleats.

Yes, I had heard fawns and does communicate with each other countless times, but never as quietly as I was hearing it that evening. Curious, I slowly reached up and removed the unit from my ear.

The deer stayed around for a few more minutes, but I never again heard a sound, although I am sure the doe and her fawns continued to communicate. I simply could not hear them without the amplification provided by the Game Ear.

That evening was another reminder to me that white-tailed deer are not the mute, silent creatures we often picture.

Although the snort could be effective in bringing a deer closer, those situations are rare, because snort sounds are stress signals to other whitetails.

Bleats and Grunts

When it comes to calling deer, bleats and grunts are the most effective sounds. We'll look at each in detail in the next couple of chapters, but let's cover some of the basics here so that we can get into the how-to, when-to and where-to stuff in later chapters.

Operating a grunt call or a bleat call is simple. So simple, in fact, that rarely do I meet anyone who actually practices with a deer call. After all, what's to practice? You put the thing to your lips, blow and — voila — you get a nice grunt or a soft bleat. Who needs to practice something so simple?

I chuckle when thinking that the same hunters who drive family and friends bonkers while learning to call elk or tuning turkey calls won't touch a deer call until they need it. That's a mistake. Although deer communicate with three basic vocalizations — the bleat, grunt and snort, with the snort being of little importance in calling — it's important to recognize variations of the bleat and grunt. Once you recognize the subtle differences in bleats and grunts, practice on the call until you can mimic these sounds the first time you blow the call for deer. Many callers can get it right on the second, third or fourth try, but by then they

If a fawn doesn't respond to the doe's simple, soft reassurance bleat, the calls become a little louder and more intense.

might have ruined the opportunity. When I'm in the woods with a call, I want to be familiar enough with it that if I want a soft grunt, I can get a soft grunt the first time, every time. This results in calling more deer. I know it did for me.

The Importance of Tone

When I was growing up, if I heard my mother say, "Gary, would you please come here, honey?" I dropped whatever I was doing to see what Mom wanted. But if I heard her say the more common, "Gary Lee Clancy! Get your butt over here this instant!" I knew I was in trouble. The words were pretty much the same, but the tone, pitch and inflection of her voice, not to mention the intensity of the words, were starkly different.

The same thing happens in the whitetail's world. Some doe bleats, for instance, are simply soft reassurances to the fawns that tell them all is well, and that mama is still looking out for them. If the fawns don't respond, the bleat becomes a little louder and more intense. There is also the bleat that says "I'm scared" or "I'm hurt." And there is a bleat that says "I'm in heat and need to breed; like right now, buster!"

If the only bleat call I can make is a simple "baaaaah," I'm missing out on a lot of opportunities with my bleat call.

The same is true of the grunt call. The things are too easy to use. I'm convinced that if they were not so easy to use, hunters would take more time to practice with them. That might cause hunters to learn the various grunts and, consequently, they would see their calling success skyrocket. We'll talk more about this in the chapter, "Using The Grunt Call."

What About Snorts?

Some specialized situations might call for a snort call. This is often referred to as a grunt-snort-wheeze in research, but as a snort-wheeze by most hunters. This could be effective in bringing a deer closer, but those situations are rare. All snort sounds are stress signals to other whitetails. The snort-wheeze, for example, means there is one very agitated buck nearby. In whitetail language, it probably means: "This is your last

Once you recognize the subtle differences in bleats and grunts, practice until you can mimic these sounds the first time you blow the call for deer.

> *If a deer blows loudly once or twice and then shuts up, you've been identified as a danger. After warning every other deer of its discovery, which is the purpose of the snort, the deer that issued the warning is now fleeing.*

chance to turn tail and run, buster! I'm about to kick some butt!" Although deer can be attracted to nearly any sound out of curiosity, it's rare for a deer to move closer to the sound of a snort-wheeze. In fact, most deer, including most bucks, will turn and flee when they hear a snort-wheeze. The exception might be a mature, dominant buck, that upon hearing the snort-wheeze, just has to investigate to see who's foolishly challenging his turf.

The same thing goes for loud snorts (blowing), which all but the neophyte hunter has heard, unfortunately. If a deer blows loudly once or twice and then shuts up, you can bet you have been identified as a danger. After warning every other nearby deer of its discovery, which is the purpose of the snort, the deer that issued the warning is now fleeing.

Sometimes, however, deer will hang around while blowing and snorting for a long time. These deer will often not stay in one spot, but will slowly circle your position, loudly snorting the whole time. They've either gotten a glimpse of you or perhaps picked up just a whiff of your scent, but they have not seen or smelled enough to positively identify the danger. They blow and snort not only to warn other deer, but to try to get you to move so they can identify the possible threat.

When I was growing up, I believed every snort was made by a buck, because all of the old-timers referred to every snort as a "buck snort." Sorry boys, but if I had a $100 bill for every doe that has snorted at me, I would be a wealthy man. In fact, research has shown that bucks tend to snort only once or twice and then vamoose, while does might hang around, circling and snorting incessantly.

CHAPTER 3

Selecting a Grunt Call

When you consider that grunt calls just caught on with hunters in the late 1980s, it's amazing to see how quickly manufacturers responded with a mind-boggling array of styles, models and innovations in these calls.

Today's deer hunters literally hundreds of different models to choose from. Is there a difference in grunt calls, or are they all pretty much alike? And if there are differences, what features should you seek in a grunt call?

To answer the first question: You bet there are differences in grunt calls. I've tried some that would make great duck calls, but they're lousy for imitating a deer's grunt calls. Some are too "tinny" and others too "reedy." And then there are a bunch of grunt tubes that do an impressive imitation of a deep grunt from a mature buck, which sounds good, but that isn't always what you want to imitate.

What to Look For

Here are the features I look for in a grunt call:

✓ Easy to blow. If it takes a big puff of wind to make the thing grunt, you won't be able to call softly. A call that can't make soft, quiet grunts will cost you deer. Only an easily blown call gives you the versatility to deal with various field conditions. On dead quiet days, you'll turn a buck inside out if you issue a loud grunt at close quarters.

✓ Good volume. This might sound like a contradiction, but even though I want a call that is easy to blow and allows me to call softly, I also want to be able to really belt one out when I'm trying to dial long distance. If a buck is far across a field, over a ridge, or even fairly close on a windy day, you'll need a versatile call so you can increase the volume for any situation. Unfortunately, some calls "shut-off" when you blow hard on them.

✓ Adjustable. For years, I carried three grunt tubes. One was for making those soft, quiet contact grunts and even quieter doe grunts. Another was perfect for imitating the slightly higher-pitched grunt of an immature buck. And the third had a deep, resonant, guttural sound, like the grunting of a real stud buck.

Hunting in cold weather requires a call that is less likely to freeze up. Those that are operated by either inhaling or exhaling are best in these situations.

Adjustable calls simplify your hunt by combining several vocalizations into one tool. The MAD call pictured above is a grunt/snort-wheeze combination.

Today I carry one grunt call that does all of these things, and it does them well. On most adjustable grunt calls, you change the call's tone and pitch by moving a rubber band that puts pressure on the reed. Still a few other calls feature a plunger or finger-position points, much like a trumpet or flute. Push down one plunger and you get a soft grunt. Depress another and the grunt is deeper. Depress another and it is very deep. The same principle is at work with the finger pressure devices. They all work, but the plunger or finger-pressure systems require a little more practice to ensure you don't make the wrong sound at the wrong time. You must know what pitch you'll get without thinking about it.

✓ Cold-weather proof. I hunt a lot in the upper Midwest and Canada, where below-zero weather can hit in November and December. In that kind of weather, no call is "freeze-proof," so I always carry a spare or two. However, calls that are least likely to be rendered inoperable by cold weather are those you can operate by inhaling or exhaling.

Does One Call Stand Against the Rest?
Is there one grunt call I recommend above all others, a call with magic

A good call should be easy to use, and it should offer good volume. Whether a buck is close by or across the field, your call should be able to handle the volume requirements for various distances.

Everyone has a preference when it comes to calls, and the only way you'll develop your own top choice is to try as many as possible to see which one sounds and works best for you.

---

in its tube? Not that I know of. I've used grunt calls made by at least a dozen different companies whose names I can recall. In addition, there are probably a couple I've forgotten. While I have not called deer in with all of them, most had the potential.

Like most hunters, I tend to stick with what I know works, so many of those calls never really got a fair chance to prove themselves. Not only that, but if you ask five guys who use calls religiously, you'll probably get five different No. 1 choices. Everyone seems to have a preference, and the only way you'll develop your own top choice is to try as many as possible and see which one sounds and works best for you.

Now, heed this advice: When you find a call you really like, buy two more, because when you lose old faithful (and you will), odds are you'll discover that your favorite grunt call has already been replaced by a "new-and-improved" model.

And when that happens, you'll likely need to start the selection process all over again.

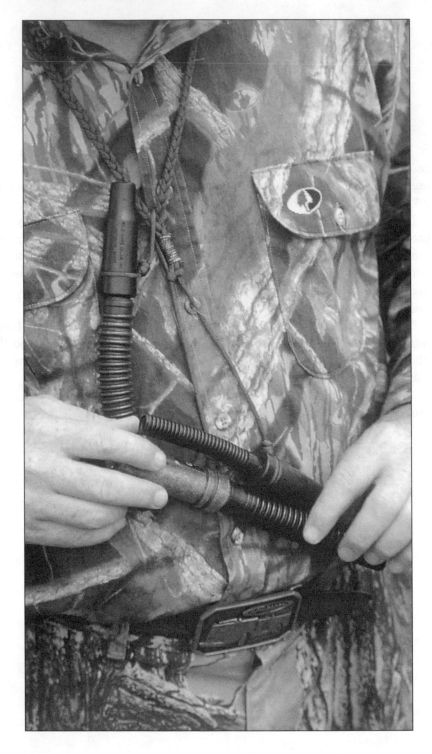

CHAPTER 4

Using the Grunt Call

Confession time: I'm a grunt-call junkie. If I have one, I have 50 of the things. Big calls, little calls, adjustable calls, some that operate with a foot pump, some that operate on friction, and still others that stick in the corner of my mouth but still allow me to shoot a bow.

I have a grunt call or two in my fanny pack and more in my day pack. I probably have an extra in each coat pocket and a bunch in my truck. And just in case I somehow get to the stand and find I've forgotten my grunt call, I've taught myself to do a good job grunting with my mouth.

No question about it, I'm a hopeless addict for grunt calls. Know why? Because grunt calls work. They work everywhere I've ever hunted and probably in all of the places I have not. A grunt call works during the pre-rut, rut and post-rut. Not only that, but it works on little bucks, medium bucks and mega-bucks. A grunt call can be used to call in deer you otherwise might never have known existed or to coax distant deer you've spotted into range.

A grunt call is the most universal tool you can use for deer hunting. And even though I love to rattle in big bucks and admit to getting a big kick out of hunting with decoys, if I had to choose just one tool from everything we'll discuss in this book, my choice would be a grunt call.

The history of the grunt call is long and short, depending on how you want to look at it. Grunt calls have been around a long time if you take into account that Indians were using hollow wooden tubes to call deer long before Columbus and Co. stumbled ashore. Deer were an important food for American Indians, who had to call deer close enough to be killed with hand-crafted bows and arrows. So, from that standpoint, calling deer is certainly not new.

But centuries passed before the first commercial deer calls — like the old Herter's call my father brought home one day — hit the market. Actually, "hit" is too strong of a term. "Languished" might better describe its revival. A few companies made a few deer calls during the 1960s and '70s, but it wasn't until the mid-1980s, when a Louisiana call-maker named Eli Haydel and a couple of Kentucky boys named Knight and Hale, began producing — and advertising — their "new" grunt calls.

Soon after, calling began to catch on with many hunters. Today, every major game-call manufacturer has several deer calls in its lineup, and dozens

Although deer make several types of grunts, if you know when and how to make the contact grunt, the trailing grunt and the tending grunt you will have the bases well covered. Some calls, like this one from Woods Wise, produce buck and doe grunts.

The contact grunt in the whitetail's world is like us saying "hello." There is no aggression involved, and it does not appear to be a territorial response.

of small call-makers offer deer calls, too.

My history with grunt calls goes back nearly 40 years. I was 10, maybe 11 years old, when my father bought a deer call from the old Herter's store in Waseca, Minn. No doubt the device had been "tested in deepest, darkest Africa by George and Jacque Herter." Of course, everything in the store had been, it seemed. Pa preferred hunting ducks and pheasants to deer, but he knew of my budding passion for whitetails, so when he spotted the deer call he bought it for me. The call was a hardwood block about the size of a candy bar, with a brass plate screwed to the block. The edge of the brass plate extended over the edge of the wood by maybe one-eighth inch. By dragging the striker, which was checkered to give it a rough finish, across the edge of the brass you could make a grunt. This peg was brass, I believe, and slightly smaller than a ball-point pen. I sure wish I still had that call, but somewhere over the years it disappeared.

At the time Pa bought me that Herter's call, I had never hunted deer. In fact, there were not many deer in our area. Spotting one while riding the school bus was enough to nearly capsize the bus as everyone shifted to one side to get a look at the rare creature. A state park wasn't far from our home, however, and it had a good deer herd. Pa would drop me off at the park on Saturday mornings before he went to work, and I would spend the day stalking, tracking and watching deer. I don't know why I was so fascinated with the whitetail from an early age, but I just could not seem to get enough of them. I still can't.

I wish I could tell you I used that Herter's call to bring in rut-crazed bucks, but that would be a lie. It was many years later that I heard what we now call a tending grunt. My trips to the park took place in the spring, summer and dead of winter. In fall, the time when I would almost surely have heard a buck or two grunting at the park, Pa and I were busy on Saturdays hunting squirrels, ducks and pheasants. But because I delighted in crawling in among the deer, I often heard the soft grunts made by bucks and does in their normal conversation. These grunts are of such low volume that unless you have good hearing and are close, you might never hear them. I got so I could mimic the soft grunts on my Herter's call. The only deer I recall coming in were button

This buck fell for a contact grunt early during bow season. One of the positive aspects of calling is that it works from opening day right up to the final minute of the season.

*I've seen many bucks on the trail of a hot doe grunt
each time a front hoof hit the ground. Others are not so
rhythmic in their grunting.*

bucks, which are inherently curious critters anyway. They probably would
have responded to a peacock call just as well! However, the excitement I felt
when I called in those nubbin bucks was as intense as the feeling I get today
when a big buck turns to my call.

Three Grunts You Should Know
Although deer make several types of grunts, if you know when and how to
make the contact grunt, the trailing grunt and the tending grunt, you will
have the bases well covered. Let's look at these basic grunts.

The Contact Grunt
Bucks — and does, to a much lesser extent — make the contact grunt at
all times of the year. During the hunting season, the contact grunt is usually
the best grunt to use early in the pre-rut and late in the post-rut. I say
"usually," because I've had bucks ignore or fail to respond to a contact grunt,
but then called them in with a trailing tending grunt. Of course, that should
not be too surprising. Each deer reacts differently at different times. In addition, from the time a buck sheds his antler velvet until the day he drops his
antlers, he is capable of breeding. Even though it might be weeks or months
before or after the peak of breeding, a buck knows what a tending grunt or
trailing grunt signals.

I know hunters who refuse to use either of these rut calls anytime but
during the rut. They're convinced a buck knows something is fishy if it hears
a tending or trailing grunt outside the rut's peak. Hey, I give the whitetail a
lot of credit, but not that much. If deer were that smart, they would be hunting us!

The contact grunt in the whitetail's world is like us saying "hello." A buck
will grunt for no apparent reason and you never know when or if a buck is
going to make a contact grunt. But when a buck hears another buck make a
contact grunt, it will often wander over to check out the buck it heard. There
is no aggression involved, and it does not appear to be a territorial response.
Bucks, like all deer, are curious critters, and it might just want to find out the
caller's identity.

The most vocal bucks I've encountered, and all those that produced weird grunts, were bucks that were actively keeping tabs on their doe.

The contact grunt is a short, soft, low-volume grunt. The best I can do in print to imitate it is this: "uurrp." Nothing harsh, and very low key. The contact grunt is most effective when used on bucks that are in sight, but out of range.

The Trailing Grunt

This is the grunt most hunters know best. The trailing grunt is often called the tending grunt or the two are commonly lumped together. There are differences, and it pays to know those differences. The trailing grunt, as the name indicates, is made by bucks trailing an estrous doe. In some cases the doe is in sight of the buck, but more often, the buck is walking nose to the ground and scent-trailing a hot doe.

The trailing grunt, like the contact grunt, is short. However, it is louder and usually repetitious. You can hear the buck's excitement and intensity in the grunt. I've seen many bucks on the trail of a hot doe grunt each time a front hoof hit the ground. Others are not so rhythmic in their grunting. They cut loose with a few grunts every 10 or even 100 yards. And I've seen bucks that acted as if they were trailing a hot doe, but did not grunt at all while within my hearing range.

This all means there is no right or wrong way to mimic the trailing grunt. Go ahead and be creative. Just remember to make it short, semi-loud and somewhat intense. When calling blind, which means no deer is in sight, I usually go with something like this: "uurp—uurrp—uurp—uurp-uurp— uurp—uurp—uurp—uurp—uurp—uurp—uurp—uurp." I might keep it up for 20 or more grunts.

Because the trailing grunt is made by deer on the move, I slowly swivel my head while calling. I start by looking over my right shoulder, begin a series of trailing grunts and end with the call's tube pointing over my left shoulder. If I'm calling to a deer I can see, I call only until I have its attention.

The Tending Grunt and the Click

The tending grunt is a very guttural grunt. Sometimes it is virtually indis-

Calling is especially valuable for hunters who need to coax the deer into close range for a clean shot.

Never grunt at a buck when he's alert and walking straight at you. If you do, the buck will typically pinpoint your location and know something isn't quite right.

Perhaps the clicking sound is a buck's way of communicating to the doe that he is the only one for her. I don't know and neither does anyone else.

---

tinguishable from the trailing grunt, and at other times I've heard bucks tending does utter grunts I would have never believed if I had not been there to see it with my own eyes and hear it with my own ears. The difference I believe is not so much with individual bucks, but with the excitement level of the buck at the moment. For example, a buck that has been trailing a doe for a long way and has just caught up to her might continue to make the trailing grunt even though he is now walking with his nose touching the doe's tail. The doe might lead the buck on in this manner for hours before finally standing for him.

The most vocal bucks I've encountered, and all those that produced weird grunts, were actively keeping tabs on their doe. When a buck wants to keep a doe in one small area, his actions remind me of a cutting horse. Each time the doe tries to make a break, the buck counters with a dash to cut her off. If another buck tries to move in, the buck puts the run on the intruder and then dashes back to his doe. During all of this, the buck might be grunting, but usually you'll hear him grunting or "clicking." I'll soon give you more on clicking.

The best example I can offer on how tending grunts can vary occurred in western Wisconsin. I had a huge buck within 60 yards several times and inside of 40 once, but I never had him where I felt confident launching an arrow. The massive buck was tending a doe, which, like most females, was playing hard to get. He would not let the doe out of his sight, and several times he ran off smaller bucks that tried to slip in on his doe that morning. The buck's tending grunts sounded like an old 3-horsepower Johnson outboard I had back in my high-school days. Not before or since have I heard a grunt similar to the extremely long, unbroken "urururuuruuruururururururururururu" of this buck. When trying to demonstrate the grunting for friends, I run out of air long before the time the buck needed another breath. That unbroken grunt went on for a minute or longer!

It's hard to go wrong when making a tending grunt, because there are so many different variations of it. Experiment and play around with different combinations. Believe me, the deer won't criticize.

Clicking, I believe, is a part of the tending grunt with some bucks and so it doesn't deserve separate treatment. At least I've never heard a buck clicking

Bucks don't always click as part of the tending grunt. In fact, I would say that probably only 20 percent of the bucks I've seen tending a doe and making the tending grunt also used clicks.

that was not tending a doe. Bucks don't always click as part of the tending grunt. In fact, I would say that probably only 20 percent of the bucks I've seen tending a doe and making the tending grunt also used clicks. I also know some good hunters who spend a lot of time in trees during the rut who have never heard a buck click.

The first five or six times I heard bucks make the clicking sound, other bucks were hanging around trying to get in on the action. I first assumed the clicking was a sound of aggression toward the other buck. It might be, but I've since seen and heard bucks making the click when no other bucks were around — or at least none that I saw. Perhaps the click is a buck's way of communicating to the doe that he is the only one for her. I don't know and neither does anyone else I've heard from, but I do know when one buck hears another buck clicking, he knows there is a doe in the picture.

That makes the click an excellent call, and it's easy to make. Just put a grunt call to your lips and say tuck or tick. I mix a few clicks in with my tending grunts. Something like this: "uurrp—uurrppp—Click-Click—uurrrpp-uurrp—Click—Click—Click—uurrrp." I will keep repeating the sequence for 15, 30, 45 seconds, maybe even a minute, whatever I feel like. Like I said, it's hard to go wrong when imitating tending grunts or clicks, because each buck is different.

One last comment concerning clicking. All the bucks I've seen and heard making the click have been mature bucks. That doesn't mean younger bucks never click. They might, but I've never heard them. When I say "mature buck," I'm not necessarily speaking of bucks 3 years and older, which is the commonly accepted age for mature status. In some regions, if does had to depend on 3-year-olds and older bucks to do all the breeding, most does would die without having been bred. In these areas — regions where 75 percent to 90 percent of the antlered bucks are killed each deer season — a 2-year-old buck is usually at the top of the pecking order, simply because bucks older than that don't exist or make up a tiny fraction of the buck herd.

Calling On the Corners
Buck Gardner is widely regarded as the master when it comes to running a

---

A white-tailed deer is not quite as good at pinpointing the exact source of a sound as is a wild turkey or any predator, but he's no slouch.

---

duck call. The man has won nearly everything there is to win in the world of duck-calling contests. But it's the marshes, rice fields and flooded timber where he's most at home. About now, you're probably looking again at the cover of this book to make sure you didn't buy a duck-hunting book by mistake, but bear with me. I'll get right back to deer. When instructing others on the fine points of calling ducks, Buck stresses what he calls, "calling on the corners." That means you never want to blow a duck call when ducks are headed right at you. If you do, ducks can pinpoint the source of the sound, and when they realize the quacking and chuckling is coming from the cattails where you're hiding instead of the decoys in front of you, they'll flare. Always call when the ducks are flying away from you or banking for the turn, i.e., the corners. For calling whitetails, all I can say to that is, "ditto."

A white-tailed deer, in my experience, is not quite as good at pinpointing the exact source of a sound — in this case a call or rattling antlers — as is a wild turkey or any predator, but he's no slouch. If you try to call to a deer that is facing you, odds are excellent the deer will focus its attention right where you don't want it: on you. You don't have to wait until the buck walks away or turns to leave, but wait until it at least turns its head before making your next call. That might sound elementary, but I can't tell you how many times I've made the mistake of blowing a call or tickling the tines when a deer was focused in my direction.

When a buck that has heard your call is standing there with ears cupped forward, staring intently in your direction, you know it's waiting to confirm what it heard. The buck wants to see the deer or at least hear the deer again. It's difficult not to give in to the temptation and give the buck what it wants. This is where patience comes in. Just sit tight and wait it out. About half the time the buck — after what seems an agonizing eternity — will flick its tail and continue its approach. But if the buck loses interest or grows suspicious and turns to leave, hit the call.

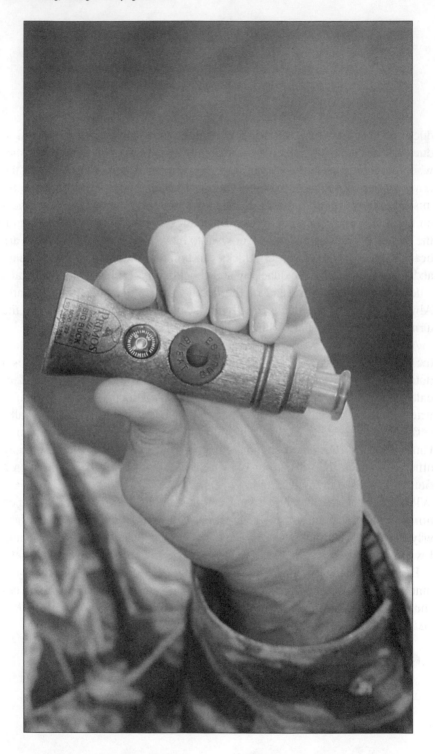

CHAPTER 5

Those "Other" Deer Calls

For many years I wrote off all calls but the grunt call as gimmicks. Oh, I tried some of those other calls, half-heartedly, I admit. And nothing happened. Just as I knew it wouldn't. So I went back to relying solely on my grunt call. After all, I knew it worked.

Then I was invited to hunt western Illinois in early November with some representatives of Woods Wise Products. If not for this hunt, I might never have learned how effective some of those "other" calls could be. This was an especially memorable event, because I absolutely didn't believe in the other calls at the time.

When we were all in camp the first afternoon, Jerry Peterson, president of Woods Wise, gave us samples of all the company's deer calls. Then he showed us how to use the calls, and we went hunting. I left most of the calls in the gift box and stuck the box under my bunk. I took only a straight buck-grunt tube and the Buc-N-Doe, a double-duty call that could be worked from either end. At the time I hung that call around my neck, I had no plans to use the end that produced doe grunts and bleats.

On the hunt's second day, I sat in a stand that was out of the loop. I'm sure you've had a similar experience. I saw five bucks that day, but all of them were cruising an oak-studded hill across a ditch and small field from where I was sitting. All were within 200 yards of my stand. With a skiff of snow covering the ground, I could see them easily, but none ventured my way. And because of a brutal, howling northwesterly wind, the bucks could not hear my grunt call or the rattling antlers I was pounding in a desperate attempt to get their attention.

By the end of the day I was wishing I had moved my stand across that field earlier, but then, the stand I was on was in a great spot. It was surrounded by big rubs and muddy scrapes, but it was not the place to be that day.

Crafting a New Plan

After sitting all day in a cold wind, I was beaten. Even so, when the last minute of legal shooting time clicked off, I climbed down, hiked back to my pickup, grabbed a stand and hustled back to find the tree I

The snort-wheeze is made by bucks when they're in a bad frame of mind. When a buck makes a snort-wheeze, you can bet another buck is involved. One of two things are about to happen. Either the other buck turns and slinks off or there is going to be a fight. Either way, the author hasn't found many times when a snort-wheeze would have improved his situation.

> *"The soft doe bleat and doe grunt are sounds every deer hears from birth. It means everything is all right. Mama is right here."*
>
> *— Gary Sefton*

had pinpointed while watching those five bucks. I hung the stand, returned to camp, wolfed down supper and fell into bed dog-tired but confident about my chances the next morning.

When I stepped outside the trailer the next morning, my confidence soared even higher. The black November sky was studded with a million diamond chips, and just the slightest hint of a breeze remained from the previous day's big blow. I forced down a big bowl of oatmeal, wished the others good luck, and jumped into my pickup. I wanted to be settled into my stand before the first glimpse of daylight.

Everything was perfect until I reached my stand. I was tying my bow to the pull-up rope when a loud snort shattered the quiet. The deer blew again and again and again. It was close, maybe only 75 yards away. Even though I could not see the deer, I was pretty sure it was a doe. No doubt bucks also snort and blow, but they tend to blow once and then get out of Dodge! Does, however, can be as nagging as a Northern red squirrel and make life miserable for an intruding hunter.

"Ain't this just dandy," I thought. "That old biddy is going to warn every deer within a mile that they better not come anywhere near here."

Calming 'er Down

My first thought was to cut across the field and sit in the stand I had hunted the previous day, but then I remembered that double-ended call around my neck. Gary Sefton, public relations manager for Woods Wise, is one of the best multi-species game callers in the country. He had told me that one of his favorite uses for the doe bleat and soft doe grunt was to use them as "calm down" calls.

"The soft doe bleat and doe grunt are sounds every deer hears from birth," Sefton said. "It means everything is all right. Mama is right here. Even a mature deer never forgets the comforting sound of a soft doe grunt or doe bleat. That's why they're excellent calls for when a deer hears you, or maybe caught a glimpse of you, but hasn't positively identified you."

It's a good idea to mix in a few tending estrous bleats along with tending grunts and trailing grunts. One way to do this is with a "call-in-a-can."

That was the situation I was facing. The doe had heard me coming, but not until I stopped at the tree did she get really nervous. The breeze was in my favor, so she had not smelled me. And even a deer cannot see well enough in the dark to identify the human form in thick timber at any distance. But she was suspicious and persistently annoying. I took the call and made a soft doe bleat, and then another.

Then I stood by the tree and listened. I could hear the deer shuffling around in the leaves ahead of my stand. Judging by the sound of the shuffling, I could tell there was more than one deer — a doe with fawns, I figured. The doe did not snort again. I started up the tree with the call in my mouth. Each time I reached another tree step, I gave a soft bleat. When I reached my stand, I fastened my safety harness, hung my day pack and pulled up my bow while issuing more soft bleats. Then I sat down, gave another bleat and waited for shooting light to seep into the timber.

It was still too dark to see them with the naked eye, but a few minutes after I got settled into my stand I could use my ears to

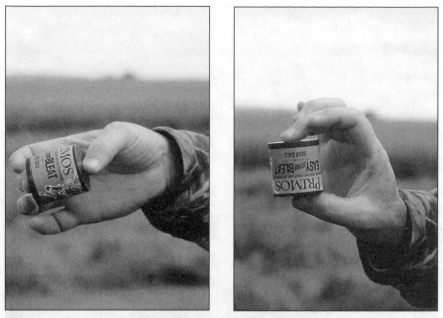

To work a "call-in-a-can," simply turn the can over. Each time you do so, the call will emit a real-sounding estrous bleat. This estrous bleat is louder and more intense than a normal doe bleat.

pinpoint their location. Later, I could see the doe and her twin fawns nonchalantly shuffling through the leaves for acorns about 100 yards in front of my stand. An hour later, when the sun crested the high ridge to the east and bathed the sidehill with meager warmth, the doe and her fawns bedded for a morning snooze in a patch of brush 30 yards from my tree.

That hunt took place in the mid-1990s, and countless times since I have used the soft doe bleat or an equally soft doe grunt to get disturbed deer calmed down.

Don't misunderstand me. This call will not calm deer that have seen enough to identify you as a hunter, and it will not convince a deer that has smelled you that its nose was wrong. And if you rattle tree stand chains or rip Velcro — sounds a deer cannot confuse with natural woodland noises — the doe bleat won't save you. But in situations like the one I just described, the doe bleat can save the day.

By the way, all my efforts that day weren't rewarded with a big buck. I saw two bucks that morning, but never fired a shot. Such is hunting.

A combination call allows a hunter to instantly adjust to the situation at hand. With simple adjustments, hunters can produce sounds from fawn bleats to buck grunts.

Come on Over

The soft doe bleat can also be used to persuade does or fawns to come closer, so it can be useful when you're hunting for antlerless deer. A perfect example took place just a mile from my front door one year. Like many regions these days, parts of Minnesota have too many deer, or at least too many as far as farmers, motorists and foresters are concerned. For several years, bow-hunters in my home area could purchase two additional antlerless-only tags in addition to the regular archery license which is an either-sex tag.

Early in the season, I was sitting one evening in a stand in a small woodlot when a group of deer began working toward me. I'm not sure how many deer there were because the thick cover prevented me from seeing all of them at once. I suspected it was the same family group of

A soft doe bleat can be used to persuade does and fawns to come closer, so it can be useful when you're hunting for antlerless deer.

does and fawns I had seen a couple of times already that season. It looked like they would walk underneath my stand, but then they suddenly veered off and followed a creek just out of bow range.

I put the call to my lips and gave a soft doe bleat. The deer I could see either didn't heard my call or ignored it. I was getting ready to call again when the matriarch doe stepped out of thick cover and walked toward my stand. Her ears were cupped forward, and she was obviously looking for the "doe" she had heard. She was 20 yards and broadside when my broadhead flashed through the top of her heart.

Mixing it Up

I often mix in a few so-called estrous bleats with my tending grunts or trailing grunts. You can do this by using two calls and quickly

Aspiring big-buck hunters must learn how to master grunt calls before they can expect to consistently kill mature bucks. Success hinges on not only knowing when to call, but which types of calls to make. Learn them all, and you'll be on your way to getting up close and personal with big bucks.

exchanging a doe-bleat call for a grunt call and then back to the grunt call again. Or you can use one of those "calls-in-a-can" as I call them. These are nifty little canisters made by companies such as Primos and Quaker Boy. To use these calls, turn them upside down and then back again, and they produce an authentic estrous bleat.

The estrous bleat is louder and more intense than a normal doe bleat. It's supposed to be made by a doe that is ready to breed, but whenever I've heard does make this sound, they've been playing hard to get, avoiding a buck's advances, and squirming away when bucks get too close. It's open for discussion whether the sound is one that does use to signal breeding readiness or to express displeasure while being harassed. Regardless, there's no debating the fact that mixing estrous bleats with trailing and tending grunts can inspire a buck to respond quickly.

Fawn In Distress

Fawns mew often, but you must be close and have excellent hearing to detect it. The mew is the fawn's way of staying in touch with its

---

The fawn bawl is a good call to use if you're looking for a fat doe for the freezer. But when a doe responds to the call, she can be difficult to shoot because she often arrives quickly and agitated.

---

mother and other deer in the family group. Chances are, the mew is the youngster's version of the bleat. Because the mew is so soft and can only be heard by deer nearby, it's of no use for calling.

But when a fawn gets into trouble, it cuts loose with a blood-curdling bawl that will make your neck hairs stand up. Does often rush to the fawn's aid. That makes the fawn bawl a good call to use if you're looking for a fat doe for the freezer.

However, when a doe or several does respond to the call, they arrive in a hurry and are extremely agitated. Trying to get one to stand still long enough to loose an arrow is difficult. Even more difficult is the fact that when a doe comes into the fawn bawl, she's on full alert. For all she knows, she could be rushing in to defend her fawn from a pack of dogs or coyotes — critters that could easily kill her as well. Deer in this high-strung category are prime candidates for "jumping the string" and ducking your arrow. In fact, after two marginal hits caused by does that jumped the string after racing to the fawn bawl, I've given up on the call. I was fortunate to recover both deer, but I'm not willing to take the chance that my luck will continue. Besides, even when you're fortunate enough to recover the deer, off-target hits caused by deer jumping the string is not what bow-hunting is all about.

When to Bawl

I've often heard the fawn bawl is most effective early in bow season, when fawns are still young and vulnerable, and the doe's maternal instincts are keen. There's probably some truth to this. Back when I used a fawn bawl to call deer, I used it as an early-season-only tool. However, I suspect the fawn bawl is more effective throughout the season than most hunters realize.

I base this belief on my observations as a coyote hunter. In winter I spend a lot of time calling coyotes. My favorite coyote call is the fawn bawl. I figure a coyote might not want to make a long trip and risk fighting another coyote for a scrawny rabbit. But a fawn? Now that's a feast! While using the fawn distress call to trick coyotes, I've often had

The author knows many good deer hunters who consistently kill mature bucks who do not rattle, nor do they use decoys. However, he doesn't know anyone who consistently scores on big bucks who does not use a grunt call. Not one.

deer come running. If does respond to the call in January and February — when I do most of my predator hunting — I suspect they will respond throughout the deer hunting season.

You probably noticed I've spoken only of does in this discussion of the fawn bleat call. The reason is that bucks rarely respond to this call. In fact, although I've probably called in nearly 100 deer with a fawn bleat call, not one has been an antlered buck.

Snort-Wheeze Calls

As I write this book in Summer 1999, I'm seeing many advertisements in hunting magazines touting calls that imitate the snort-wheeze of an agitated buck. This makes me wonder. In the 40 years I've been messing with white-tailed deer I cannot recall one instance where I've said to myself, "Gee, I wish I had a snort-wheeze call."

No doubt bucks also snort and blow, but they tend to blow once and then get out of Dodge! Does, however, can be as nagging as a Northern red squirrel and make life miserable for an intruding hunter.

The snort-wheeze is made by bucks when they're in a bad frame of mind. When a buck makes a snort-wheeze, you can bet another buck is involved. One of two things are about to happen. Either the other buck turns and slinks off or there is going to be a fight.

I guess some argument could be made for kicking off a rattling session with a snort-wheeze, but will a snort-wheeze make any difference in whether a buck responds to the rattling? I doubt it.

Although most deer calls are worthwhile tools to help you see more deer and get more shots at deer, I believe the snort-wheeze call is a gimmick. Of course, I know some hunters and call-manufacturers who will argue with me and recount successes they've had with this call, but as the 1900s come to a close, Gary Clancy isn't convinced.

The Old Reliable

Before moving on to rattling in the next chapter, let me leave you with this: I know many good deer hunters who consistently kill mature bucks who do not rattle, nor do they use decoys. They don't have anything against rattling or decoying, but for various reasons, they don't rely on those tactics. However, I don't know anyone who consistently scores on big bucks who does not use a grunt call. Not one.

Bill Winke, a fellow outdoor writer, is a good example. Winke lived many years in south-central Iowa, arguably one of the three or four best big-buck locales in North America. He didn't live there by chance. He lived there because of the region's whitetails and because nonresidents must rely on a drawing to get a deer tag, while residents are guaranteed one. Winke is not one to slap himself on the back, so you'll never hear about all the mature bucks he's killed. Let's just say he knows his stuff about whitetails. He says at least half of the mature bucks he's killed came to grunt calls. I can't leave you with a better reason to use a grunt call than that.

CHAPTER 6

Is Rattling Just Location and Timing?

When I give deer hunting seminars, I usually look forward to hunters coming up afterward to share their stories or to ask me more questions about the subject I was discussing.

Unfortunately, I've almost come to dread doing seminars on rattling. Why? Because even though I always discuss the importance of timing and location, some hunters can't or won't believe that a whitetail is a whitetail is a whitetail. It simply doesn't matter if a deer lives in the suburbs of Chicago or the scrub brush of South Texas.

A guy in a red shirt got things rolling.

"Good talk, but I've tried rattlin' round here, and I don't care whatcha say, it just don't work here."

All heads nodded in unison. I got that old "outnumbered again" feeling in my gut.

"Man, I've tried rattling antlers I don't know how many times," chimed in the young guy with the ponytail. "The only deer I've seen have been headin' the other way. I think rattling scares deer around here."

All heads keep nodding in unison, but I notice the intensity increasing.

Now it's time to hear from the big guy with the fresh chew.

"Just watch the huntin' videos. Where do they rattle in all the deer? Texas, that's where. Maybe a few in Canada. Ever see a video where they rattle in bucks right here in _____ (fill in the state and county of your choice)? Hell no, you ain't. Wanna know why? Cuz it don't work here, that's why."

All heads nod even faster and more enthusiastically. I'm suddenly picturing a rail, feathers and hot tar.

I've fought and lost enough battles in my life to know when I'm up against the wall.

"Well guys, I would like to continue this discussion, but I have to make room for the next speaker. Thanks for coming, and have a great show. Bye now!"

Although there's more to a balanced herd than just keeping the number of deer of each sex as close to even as possible, the doe-to-buck ratio is the most influential factor.

Believe Me, It Works. Really!

I've done seminars on rattling in a lot of places over the years, and the results are always the same. The only things that change are the faces. So why do I keep doing seminars on rattling when it appears everyone thinks I'm crazy or lying?

Allow me to explain. As I go through my slides and give my spiel, I make eye contact with the audience. I see a lot of different emotions in those eyes: boredom, stubbornness, skepticism, cynicism, sleepiness, to name a few. Sure, I've seen it all. But then I catch the eye of a young hunter who is hanging on every word. I'll also see the look of recognition in the eyes of another when I talk about the sheer excitement of having a buck come to the horns. I figure if only a few of the hunters in the audience can experience the adrenaline rush I get every time a buck comes to the clashing antlers, then putting up with all the non-believers is a small price to pay.

Looking back through a lifetime of daily log books, I've discovered I've been fortunate enough to have hunted whitetails in 17 states and provinces. In 12 of the 17, I have rattled in bucks. If you wish to omit South Texas and Saskatchewan from the list, that still leaves 10 states in which I've had bucks come to my rattling attempts.

Furthermore, in none of these cases was I hunting behind a high fence. About half of the bucks I've rattled in have been on public land. The other half were on private land where I had permission to hunt. Because I do not own a set of magic horns, I'm betting that if I can rattle in bucks in Minnesota, Wisconsin, Illinois, Michigan, Mississippi, Georgia, South Dakota, Missouri, Saskatchewan and Texas, you can probably rattle in bucks wherever you hunt, too. Latitude and longitude are not the determining factors when it comes to rattling success.

Doe-to-Buck Ratios

So why is it that if you're fortunate enough to hunt a good ranch in South Texas about mid-December when the rut kicks into high gear, you can expect to rattle in more bucks in one day than you will during an

This buck was rattled in on a foggy morning in South Texas by the author and John Pflueger. They had been working on filming a segment for a Realtree Monster Buck video.

entire season or maybe a lifetime elsewhere?

The No. 1 reason is herd dynamics, or what we commonly call the doe-to-buck ratio. Although there's more to a balanced herd than just keeping the number of deer of each sex as close to even as possible, the doe-to-buck ratio is the most influential factor. On the big-buck ranches of South Texas (translation: big $$$s), deer are a cash crop. The herd is managed to produce an optimum number of mature, trophy-class bucks that well-heeled hunters are willing to pay thousands of dollars for a chance to hunt. Most ranches strive for an evenly balanced doe-to-buck ratio, but rarely is a 1-1 ratio achieved, unless the ranch is high-fenced. Doe-to-buck ratios of two or three does for every buck are more common. At low ratios, competition between mature bucks for available does is intense, and it is competition that prods a buck into responding to the clash of antlers.

The Role Of Hunting Pressure

Light hunting pressure is another major factor that contributes to South Texas' reputation as a mecca for rattling in big bucks. Rarely will

This Saskatchewan buck is the largest the author has ever taken. The buck responded to rattling antlers on a brutally cold morning in mid-November. Cold, clear days that follow on the heels of a cold front are the author's favorite time for rattling.

What's interesting about late-estrous encounters is that even though I've often seen two or more bucks pursuing the same female, I've only witnessed one buck fight during this period.

a buck be so pumped up on testosterone that it will throw all caution to the wind when a hunter lurks behind every fifth tree. As hunting pressure increases, your odds of rattling in a buck start nose-diving. On top ranches in South Texas, bucks don't know the definition of hunting pressure.

One day while hunting The Perlitz Ranch in South Texas, we were telling hunting stories during a lunch break. My good friend Greg Miller and I got to telling the rest of the group what it's like on opening day of deer season in our home states of Minnesota and Wisconsin. I could tell by the faces of the Perlitz brothers, Jimmy and Stuart, that we might just as well have been talking about deer hunting on Mars. Having lived and hunted in South Texas all of their lives, they couldn't fathom the scenes Miller and I described. On ranches like the Perlitz's, hunter numbers are so strictly controlled that hunting pressure is a nonfactor. When you talk numbers like one hunter per week for each 5,000 to 10,000 acres, the term "hunting pressure" becomes obsolete.

Two Prime Times to Rattle

Weather also plays a role in rattling success. Given a choice of weather conditions, I prefer one of those cold, clear days that follow right on the heels of a cold front. I also like the unsettled weather that generally precedes such a cold front. If the rut is on, bucks will be on the move, and bucks on the move are prime candidates for rattling action.

The biggest whitetail I've ever rattled in and killed was taken on just such a morning. The temperature was 23 degrees below zero, which is a little nippier than I like it, but that buck was hot!

Another time, while hunting at Willow Point — an island in the Mississippi River between Louisiana and Mississippi — a severe cold front pushed through. The temperatures plunged into the single digits overnight, which is mighty cold for that part of the country in mid-December. The next morning, with a heavy frost covering everything and not a hint of wind, I rattled in seven bucks before 10 o'clock. That's when I had to leave to catch the ferry back to the mainland. Three of

Afternoon usually means less deer movement. It's not that deer won't come to your rattling in the afternoon, but morning is much more effective. The two times don't even compare.

If I'm hunting an area where I'm restricted to a small piece of land, I don't bother to rattle in the afternoons, because I don't want to risk ruining the site for the next morning.

those bucks, two 6-pointers and a forkhorn, came in together and frantically ran in circles around the tree where I was perched. It was almost comical watching them try to find the source of the rattling they had heard. I didn't want to climb down at 10 a.m. to leave, but I had a plane to catch.

Running a close second to those frigid conditions would be a day with mist, light rain, falling snow or even fog. Again, such weather tends to encourage buck movement.

While hunting on the Encinido's Ranch in South Texas one year, guide John Pflueger — who is one of the best at shaking antlers — and I rattled in 13 bucks in one morning. The fog was so thick we could not see the deer until they were well within range of the Knight muzzleloader I was using. Cameraman Randy "Stomper" Marcum captured it all on video for Realtree Outdoors' Monster Buck series. I also have a very clear copy in my hunter's memory banks. Although some of the bucks we rattled in that morning were respectable, none were the buck Pflueger had seen a few days before. He had described it to me in detail before we set out that morning. Marcum, who wanted to get a good kill on video, encouraged me to shoot a couple of times, but I held out for the big 10-pointer Pflueger had assured me had to be in the neighborhood. About noon, the hot Texas sun melted the fog and our success with the horns dropped to zero, so we knocked off for the afternoon.

That occurrence is common wherever I've hunted whitetails. It's not that you cannot rattle in bucks during the afternoon, but morning tends to be much more productive. In fact, the two don't even compare. If I'm hunting an area where I'm restricted to a small piece of land, I don't bother to rattle in the afternoons, because I don't want to risk ruining the site for the next morning.

Even though the Encinido's Ranch has more land than you could cover in a week, Pflueger and I didn't want to tip our hand to the big 10-pointer by rattling when we knew our odds of enticing the buck into muzzleloading range was slim.

The next morning, with the fog once again blanketing the endless expanse of mesquite and cactus, we made our first set and began rattling as soon as there was enough light for the camera. The first buck to respond was the 10-pointer Pflueger had described. I killed him on camera as he circled our position in an attempt to get downwind of us. Given the conditions, I'm sure that if the big buck had not been the first one to respond that morning, we could have matched or exceeded our response numbers from the previous day.

I can hear you skeptics saying: " Ya, but that's Texas. Let's see you do that where I live!" Well, I once rattled in six bucks one Nov. 7 morning while bow-hunting in western Wisconsin. A light snow fell gently from a gray, nearly windless sky. Again, ideal conditions.

Those are my favorite weather conditions for rattling (or for deer hunting, in general), but that doesn't mean you can't rattle in bucks during less-than-ideal conditions. As long as the time is right (which we'll cover next) I'll be rattling, regardless of the weather. I've rattled in enough bucks when it was too hot, too cold or too windy for optimum rattling success that I'm not about to let weather conditions dictate whether I rattle the bones.

Even so, experience has convinced me that the best action usually occurs under one of the two conditions I have just described. Give me one of those days during prime time and I can't wait to hit the woods and start rattling.

Timing is Critical

No matter where you do your rattling, you're wasting your time if the timing is not right. Sure, you might rattle in a few bucks during the early pre-rut and again late in the post-rut, but darned few. So few, that I don't even carry rattling antlers during these times.

But when bucks begin serious scraping activity, it's time to get on the horns. The rut's scraping period normally lasts 10 days to two weeks in regions that have a short, defined rut. Rattling success just gets better and better as each day passes and the first wave of does comes into estrus. The tail end of the scraping period, when bucks are virtually beside themselves with pent up aggression and sexual frustration, is the very best time to rattle.

Some hunters believe that once actual breeding commences you can forget about rattling in bucks, but I've found that to be bad advice. While it's true that it's rare for a buck to leave a doe to check out the sounds of fighting bucks, a buck that is between does or has not found one is a prime candidate for rattling. Of course, you won't find this occurring

*Some hunters believe that once actual breeding
commences, you can forget about rattling in bucks.
But I've found that to be bad advice.*

where does outnumber bucks by 5-to-1 ratios. In those regions, bucks are so busy servicing hot does that they have no reason to respond to rattling.

I've also heard and read a thousand times that if you rattle in a buck during the rut's breeding phase it will likely be a little guy. The reasoning is that because an area's dominant buck is first in line for breeding rights, he will likely be occupied with a willing doe 24 hours a day during the rut. Therefore, it's unlikely he'll respond to rattling. While that part is true, let's not forget that an area's dominant buck is frequently not the buck with the largest antlers. Dominance in the whitetail's world is a factor of attitude, strength and body size more than rack size. It's not unusual for a 10-pointer with trophy-class headgear to play second fiddle to an 8-pointer with a respectable rack. This typically means a buck with a larger, more muscular body and an attitude that reminds us of a middle linebacker in the old-time NFL.

Never underestimate the importance of attitude. Just as with humans, some deer are more aggressive than others. It's not uncommon for a real bully of a younger buck to claim the No. 1 position over an older but less aggressive buck, despite not being able to match the old boy's headgear.

Rattling During the Post-Rut

Another myth concerning rattling is that rattling anytime during the post-rut period is a waste of time. I disagree. It's worth giving it a try during the first week to 10 days of the post-rut. Even though most of the does have been bred, a few will come into estrus late. Besides, bucks don't just turn the breeding-urge switch to the off position one day. It's more of a gradual turn-off, a dimmer switch, so to speak. During that first week to 10 days after peak breeding subsides, you can bet that bucks — although tiring from the rigors of the rut — can still be enticed to check out a fight just in case a hot doe is hanging around.

In fact, I know some good hunters who consider this period to be the ultimate time for rattling in top-end bucks. They accept the fact they won't rattle in lots of deer at this time, but they're willing to forgo the excitement of numbers for one glimpse of a giant.

Greg Miller, an outdoor writer from Wisconsin, is pictured here. The author has spent time with Miller on hunts in South Texas where hunting pressure is almost nonexistent.

I've often tried rattling during what is commonly called the second rut or second estrus, but I've never had much luck. A secondary rut occurs in the Midwest, where up to 60 percent of the female fawns are bred during their first year. Much of this occurs after the main rut when the fawns reach about 6 months of age. Then too, any does that were not bred or did not conceive during the first rut will cycle back in after about 28 days. Although I've seen a lot of second-rut activity over the years, I've never seen rut activity that's anywhere near as frenzied as the main rut. My theory is that even though bucks are willing to service the relatively few does that enter estrus during the second rut, their testosterone levels have subsided and they're physically run down from the main rut. As a result, they're unable or unwilling to go through all of the rituals associated with the main rut, including fighting, scraping, indiscriminate chasing of does, and answering the call of the horns. If they can mate without a whole lot of effort — out of convenience, in other words — they'll do so, but that's about it.

During this late-estrous period, because only one doe will usually be in heat at one time in any area, it's not uncommon to have several bucks quietly pursuing the hot doe or fawn. Once while hunting southern Iowa just before Christmas, I watched five mature bucks — the two largest of which would have scored in the 150s — chase a hapless female fawn all over a hillside for an hour. Once they disappeared over the hill, I continued my attempt to slip up on them. My attempt ended up memorable, but futile.

What's interesting about these late-estrous encounters is that even though I've often seen two or more bucks pursuing the same female, I've only witnessed one buck fight during this period. On that occasion, as far as I could tell, the squabble was not over a doe. The fact that several evenly matched bucks can engage in a chase without coming to blows is a sign the bucks' aggression level has greatly subsided since the peak of the main rut.

Why Do They Respond?

Why does a white-tailed buck respond to the sound of two bucks fighting? Of course, only deer know for sure, but most experienced rattlers I know agree most mature bucks respond out of pure aggression. When the rut is near or in progress, bucks have little time for other bucks. In human terms, we would call it spoiling for a fight.

I'm sure some bucks come to the sound of clashing antlers hoping to make off with the estrous doe that might be coyly waiting at ringside. Of

The author is pictured here with a buck he rattled in. Clancy has found that no matter which part of the country you hunt, rattling can be effective.

When a mature buck comes to the horns, he often strides onto the scene all stiff-legged, ears laid back, and the whites of his eyes bright and visible. A buck like this is not just there out of curiosity.

course, not every buck fight — not even most buck fights — involve a hot doe. Even so, enough fights do involve a doe that some bucks know it's worth investigating the battle scene.

Dominant bucks, especially, might respond because they might consider the fight to be a territorial infringement. Even though deer aren't considered territorial in a strict biological definition, there's no doubt a mature buck has a piece of real estate he considers his own, and woe be the buck that invades his domain. In some cases, that turf just happens to be where he is at the moment.

When a mature buck comes to the horns he often strides onto the scene all stiff-legged, ears laid back, hair bristled on the back of his neck, and the whites of his eyes bright and visible. This buck is not just there out of curiosity!

Curiosity, however, does make many bucks come to the sounds of rattling. This is especially true of young bucks. You can see by their actions that they're wondering what the fuss is about. Does and fawns will also come to rattling sometimes, in all likelihood out of curiosity.

I've also rattled in coyotes, a gray fox, a family of raccoons, an incredibly fat skunk, a flock of turkeys, a herd of Holstein cows, a few horses, assorted farm dogs and two curious farmers over the years!

CHAPTER 7

Rattling with the Real Thing

For many years, I've listened to stories about sex-crazed bucks that came charging to the rattle of chains as hunters hung tree stands. Others claimed to have rattled in bucks by tapping their aluminum arrows together, either on purpose or by accident.

And then there was my farmer friend who watched as a wild-eyed buck burst from the brush while he was mending a fence. The buck evidently was lured to the scene by the creaking of barbwire and the hammering noise as my friend drove staples into the cedar posts. The buck, his hair bristled up to make him look even bigger than he was, started doing that stiff-legged, sideways thing bucks do right before they lower the boom on another buck. My friend is not a deer hunter, but he has been around animals all of his life, and he recognized the aggression. Luckily, his tractor was just a few steps away. He quickly jumped up on the machine, which, by the way, had been idling loudly the whole time!

I listened politely to the stories, but I always took them with a grain of salt. After all, I've hung a lot of stands and rattled a lot chains in the process. I've tapped arrows together, but not on purpose. And I've even been known to put on the heavy gloves and fix a fence now and then. Well, no buck ever came to check me out while I was doing these things. I assumed they only responded to the sound of real antlers.

Well, I changed my viewpoint a few years ago when I had an experience that made me believe all of those stories. Hey guys: I apologize for ever doubting you!

It's rare that I can be found anywhere but in the deer woods every day and usually all day from mid-October to late-November. I wait all year for that six-week stretch. However, a few years ago I happened to be home for three days during the peak of the rut. Home for me is southeastern Minnesota. The firearms deer season, which coincides with the peak of the rut in Minnesota, was in full swing. I wasn't hunting because I had already used my tag on a buck during bow season.

Pheasant season was open, and because I wasn't scheduled to leave for a deer hunt in Illinois for a few days, I decided to take Meg, my little Brittany, and search for some roosters. At the time, area farmers had enrolled a substantial amount of land in the Conservation Reserve

The author changed his views on rattling after watching seven bucks respond to the sound of a bell attached to his bird dog while hunting pheasants.

Many hunters use real antlers for sentimental reasons.Whatever your reason, choose two antlers that fit your hands well, and remove the brow tines to prevent yourself from bashing your fingers and thumbs while rattling.

Program. I had access to about 2,000 acres.

Meg is a small dog, not quite coming up to my knee. Keeping track of her in CRP fields is impossible without a bell. As Meg hunts, the bell's constant "ding-da-ding-ding-ding" keeps me posted on her whereabouts. When she gets a snoot full of bird scent and slows down to work the bird, the occasional tinkling lets me home in on her location. When the bell goes quiet, I know she's locked up on point.

On the first morning, I waited until the sun evaporated the frost from the grass before heading out to hunt. The first field was just a half-mile from my home. As we approached, Meg tore off through the field like a possessed demon. We were halfway across the field and about 80 yards from the edge of a cornfield when a buck came bouncing out of the corn. At first, I thought deer hunters were driving the field and spooked the deer, but then the buck stopped and stared at Meg. It was obvious the buck was trying to pinpoint the source of the sound it had heard — the bell. The buck pranced over toward Meg.

To keep track of me, Meg occasionally jumps in a pogo-stick fashion

Rattling works best late in the pre-rut, but don't think it will never work during other times of the season. Curious bucks can sometimes be duped with rattling tactics throughout the fall.

so she can see over the top of the grass. This time, when she bounced up out of the grass, I saw her eyes go wide as she spotted the buck closing in on her. Meg instantly made a beeline back to me, with the buck right behind her. It wasn't until she was at my side that the buck saw me. He was only 30 yards away when he stopped and stared. He stared for a while before turning slowly, and reluctantly walking back into the standing corn.

During the next three days, six more bucks came to the tinkling of that brass bell! Remember, this was during the middle of the gun season. Three bucks came from standing corn, one from a slough choked with stunted willow and red osier dogwood, and two bucks popped up out of the CRP fields. Although one of the bucks was a 2½-year-old 8-pointer, all of the others were yearlings. However, seven bucks in three days was a better average than I had ever had while rattling from a tree stand. I figured the bell was magic!

When I packed my gear for Illinois, Meg's bell went with me. Talk about feeling self-conscious. There I was sitting in a tree stand in western Illinois, a deer hunting expert in the eyes of some, and what am I

Heavy antlers have a different ring to them than do thin antlers. My antlers go "CLUNK-CLUNK-CLUNK," while thin antlers go "clackety-clackety-clack." Does it make any difference to deer? Possibly not.

doing? You guessed it, ringing that little brass bell for all it was worth. Man, am I glad nobody ever saw me!

I would like to report that bucks came running from every nook and cranny of those Pike County, Ill., hills, but they didn't. Not a single deer responded to Meg's bell. Why did it work on those Minnesota pheasant hunts? Well, it wasn't the bell. Most likely, it was simply a prime time for rattling. Those bucks would have come to anything that remotely sounded like two bucks fighting.

Because I've finally made my confession on the dog bell episode after hiding that deep, dark secret all of these years, I might as well finish my confession. After the Illinois trip, I got to thinking that maybe it wasn't just the sound of the bell, but the broken cadence of the bell ringing as Meg swept though the grass that attracted those bucks. In Illinois, I had simply held the bell by the leather thong and, rather timidly, (because I felt like a damned fool) shook the bell a few times. What if I could better imitate the way the bell had sounded in the CRP fields?

A day later, I was in a tree stand in western Wisconsin. Meg's brass bell was again with me. But this time I had another tool: an ice fishing jig pole! I tied the bell to the end of the short, limber pole and filled the quiet November woods with the sound of that worn bell. Of course, nothing showed. At last, Meg got her bell back. I was now convinced it was a matter of timing and not some pied-piper quality of the bell.

This story serves a function other than cleansing my soul. The point is this: You don't need a set of real antlers to attract deer. In fact, I cannot say with any reasonable certainty that you will rattle in any more deer with a set of real antlers than you will with synthetic antlers, rattling bags or other rattling devices. However, real antlers have many advantages over other methods. Let's take a look at them.

The Real McCoy

Nothing sounds as much like the real thing as the real thing. While I have no way of knowing if a buck can recognize or cares about that authenticity, I believe that in some instances it is the difference between

Fresh antlers produce the best sounds for rattling. Avoid antlers that have been exposed to the weather for long periods, especially if they're bleached.

The author uses large antlers for rattling. He prefers antlers from racks scoring 125 to 150 inches.

a response and a no-show. What's more, real antlers can provide confidence, which is reason enough for me to carry real antlers into the woods.

When I do seminars on rattling, I take real antlers for demonstrations. People are often amazed at the size of those rattling antlers. I've never scored them, but if you stuck them on a mount and gave them a 17-inch spread, the score would probably be in the low 150s. Being an incurable romantic, the reason I started using such a big set of rattling antlers had nothing to do with function or form and everything to do with memories.

One side is a 5-point shed. This shed is from a deer I hunted hard for four seasons without ever so much as drawing my bow. The shed is from what I assume was his last winter because he was never seen again. You might suspect the shed from that buck invokes memories of the masterful chess game we played all of those years, but, that isn't the case. Instead, the shed reminds me of all the dumb mistakes I made those four seasons. Remembering those errors makes me a better hunter.

The other side is an equally impressive 5-point antler, although I have removed the brow tines from both sides to save on thumb damage. The

---

My idea of a good set of rattling antlers is something in the 125- to 150-inch class. I remove the brow tines to prevent me from bashing my fingers and thumbs while rattling.

---

buck that once wore that antler lived to the ripe age of 4½ years in the rolling, oak-studded hills of northern Missouri. My friends Tom and Shirley Benson own a renovated school house in Oxford, Mo. (population 12 — when I'm in town). They let me use the school house as my base camp when I'm hunting deer and turkeys.

On a warm, foggy mid-October morning, the sun was just trying to break through the fog when a buck, backlit by the struggling sun, suddenly appeared. I had about three seconds to see the deer, draw and release an arrow before he would have melted back into the fog. I saw the buck, saw that heavy antler, drew and released. The buck, hit through both lungs, buck ran only 50 yards before piling up. Even though I heard him crash and knew he was down for the count, it took some time before my legs would support me well enough so I could climb down from my stand. After all, with just that one glimpse, I knew the buck was going to be the best I had ever taken with bow and arrow.

When I finally climbed down, I didn't bother with the blood trail. I just walked straight to where my ears had told me the buck had crashed. I found him there lying on his right side in the bottom of what they call a ditch in Missouri — a gully most other places. The ditch had blown full of leaves and that heavy antler was completely buried in the leaves. Unfortunately, the left antler was just a broken stub. Talk about mixed emotions. The buck, of course, was no less a trophy just because he wore only one antler. He had, after all, managed to beat long odds and survive to maturity. That side of my rattling antlers takes me back to that foggy morning in Missouri and the near spiritual experience of watching that buck ooze out of the wet, gray background.

Can Sound Make a Difference?

Enough of these sentimental recollections. The hard facts are that when I mesh and grind those two heavy antlers together it sounds like two big bucks getting it on. Heavy antlers have a different ring to them than do thin antlers. My antlers go "CLUNK-CLUNK-CLUNK," while thin antlers go "clackety-clackety-clack." Does it make any difference to

Although some hunters prefer to cut the tips off the tines of their rattling antlers, the author does not. He believes the tips produce more realistic sounds, especially at the beginning of rattling sequences.

When you find a set of antlers that suits you, drill a hole through each base and run a cord through the holes. The cord should be about 30 inches long.

If you're interested in attracting big bucks, small antlers might not be the best option for rattling antlers, especially if you don't feel confident with them. Small, thin antlers do not produce the dense sounds that some hunters believe trigger responses from mature bucks.

deer? Possibly not. But then again, what if it does? What if really big bucks aren't interested in checking out the skirmishes of small bucks? What if the big boys recognize the clackety-clack sound to mean that a couple of immature bucks — which are no threat to their breeding rights — are simply fighting among themselves? When that same buck hears my antlers go CLUNK-CLUNK-CLUNK, does he possibly recognize the sound as coming from antlers worn by mature bucks? Can a buck discern the difference? If he can, is he more inclined to investigate the sound of the fight between two mature bucks, deer that might be big enough and bold enough to challenge him for breeding rights? I think so.

My idea of a good set of rattling antlers is something in the 125- to 150-inch class. I remove the brow tines to prevent me from bashing my fingers and thumbs while rattling. I prefer at least three and, better yet, four points on each antler after the brow tines are removed. More tines make it easier to mesh antlers and get that classic clatter sound. Some guys like both antlers from the same side, others prefer a set from one deer. I even know a couple of guys who use mule deer antlers for calling

The author believes big bucks respond to the sounds made by large rattling antlers because they recognize the sounds as those made by deer that might challenge them for breeding rights.

Some guys rub rattling antlers with linseed oil before each season. They believe oil keeps antlers dense and retains that "fresh" sound. I don't think this is necessary as long as you hang your antlers inside your garage and don't expose them to sun, rain and snow.

whitetails. I'm not too concerned about what types of antlers I use. I merely want them to fit my hands — not too large and not too small.

When you find a set of antlers that suits you, drill a hole through each base and run a cord through the holes. I prefer a cord that's about 30 inches long. Bleached antlers, which usually indicates they have been lying in the woods or nailed to the rafters of a barn for a long time, are poor choices for rattling. They don't have the ring to them that hard antlers have. Too much exposure to the elements makes antlers sound mushy, like punky wood.

I know some guys who rub their rattling antlers with linseed oil before each season. They believe the linseed oil keeps antlers dense and retains that "fresh" sound. I don't think this is necessary as long as you hang your antlers inside your garage and don't expose them to sun, rain and snow.

Some hunters like to cut off the tips of the tines to further reduce the chance of injuring themselves while rattling. I don't cut the tips of my antlers because I think blunting the tips makes it more difficult to begin a rattling sequence.

I begin sequences by lightly brushing the tips together, which produces authentic sounds. Again, none of this might make any difference to deer, but I figure if I'm going to go through the hassle of lugging around real antlers, I want them to sound as much like the real thing as possible.

CHAPTER 8

A Look at Plastic Noise-Makers

Synthetic antlers look like the real thing — unless they're painted red or orange for safety reasons — but they don't sound like the real thing. That doesn't mean they sound bad or deer won't respond to them. However, they definitely don't sound like real antlers.

I have proved it and so can you. Have a buddy walk out of your sight with a set of real antlers and a pair of synthetics. Tell him do five 10-second sparring sessions with each, and tell him to mix them up. While listening, use a pen and notebook to record which sessions you think are from real antlers and which ones are from fake antlers. This is an easy test. I scored 100 percent and so did two of my hunting buddies.

Even my wife, who is not a deer hunter, missed only two. If Nancy Clancy, who would much rather have been working on quilts than participating in what she calls "another one of your dumb games," can tell the difference, surely deer can tell the difference, too. The question is, does it matter?

If I'm going to carry antlers into the woods, I would just as soon carry the real thing. The advantage of alternative rattling devices like rattling bags and boxes is convenience. The only advantage of synthetic antlers is that they come ready to use: no drilling or cutting is involved. However, a set of synthetic antlers are no more or less convenient to lug around the woods than are real antlers.

Some hunters buy synthetic antlers because they don't want to cut up a big rack to make them into rattling horns. Either that, or maybe they don't have access to sheds. If that's the case, then synthetic antlers are the answer.

Rattling Bags

I like rattling bags. Maybe that's because I've rattled in a bunch of deer with these bags. When it comes to imitating the tinny "click-click-clickety-click" of early-season sparring, nothing beats a bag. Rattling bags are also excellent tools for imitating the sounds of a serious buck

Here are two styles of "plastic clackers." At left is the Lohman Double Rattle, featuring two plastic paddles. The MAD Calls rattling system, right, features a two-box design, which produces more volume. An advantage of plastic clackers is their ability to project their noise for long distances. They're especially suited for windy days.

fight. I also like the way I can work a bag with one hand when I need to keep my other hand on the gun or bow.

The original rattling bags featured round wooden dowels inside of cloth covers. These worked, but not as well as today's bags that feature synthetic dowels of different shapes and sizes. The new bags make it much easier to operate, especially with one hand.

Anyone who has done much rattling can tell you it's not uncommon for a buck to show up while the hunter is still rattling. That's why I like bags. When bow-hunting, my favorite method is to face the tree and hold my bow in my left hand and use my right hand to roll the rattling bag against the tree trunk.

When a buck appears, I just let the bag drop to my side where it hangs from its drawstring, which I usually clip to my safety harness. If the buck hangs up and needs further encouragement, I just reach down and gently work the bag.

Now that's slick!

Those Plastic Clacker Things

Lohman was the first company to offer a rattle box. The Lohman Battling Bucks System was basically a plastic paddle attached inside a plastic box.

When you shake or slap the paddle against the side of the box, you get a sound that sounds like, well, like plastic against plastic. Brad Harris is Lohman's director of public relations, and we have known each other a long time. Harris is an excellent hunter, so when he sent me a prototype and asked me to try it out, I told him I would. However,

The original rattling bags featured round wooden dowels inside of cloth covers. These worked all right, but not as well as today's bags that feature synthetic dowels of different shapes and sizes.

after I opened the box and tried it, I wished I had said no. Frankly, it sounded awful to my ears.

However, I had promised Harris I would give it a try, so when bow season opened, I took my old rattling bag out of my fanny pack and replaced it with what I called "the clacker." I'll admit I did not have much hope of it working, but then I remembered how the sound of my bird dog's collar bell once attracted six bucks during the rut. Nothing happened the first couple of times I tried the clacker. I was disap-

Rattling boxes are easy to use. To produce rattling sounds, simply slide or slap the call's plastic paddles together. These calls are especially useful for bow-hunters when bucks hang up in nearby thick cover.

Anyone who has done much rattling can tell you that it's not uncommon for a buck to show up while the hunter is still rattling. That's why I like bags.

pointed, but it was early in the season and responses during the pre-rut are limited at best, anyway.

My luck changed one evening when I heard the unmistakable sound of antlers touching antlers somewhere behind my stand. It was only once and just for a couple of seconds, but I knew the sound came from two bucks. I immediately took out the clacker, removed the rubber band and used the palm of my hand to just tickle the paddle against the sides of the box a couple of times.

I put the rubber band back on, dropped the call into the cargo pocket of my pants, grabbed my bow and waited. Within a minute, a 5-point buck stepped into a small opening behind my stand. Right behind him was a yearling 6-pointer. I didn't shoot either buck, but at least I knew the clacker was not scaring deer.

That incident gave me the confidence to use it more often. As a result, I rattled in a few more deer with it during the pre-rut. However, when the rut's scraping period began, I admit I went back to my big set of real antlers.

The Clacker Sees More Action

I hunted hard the rest of the early bow season, but didn't tag a buck. Opening day of the Minnesota firearms season found me hunting in the hill country just east of my home. Normally, hunting pressure is intense on opening weekend of the bucks-only season and, for that reason, I would never consider rattling, even though the Minnesota gun season usually falls during the peak of the rut.

I changed my mind on this opening day because, for some reason, no other hunters showed up on the farm I was hunting, and I heard only a smattering of shots in the distance.

At about 10 a.m., I was slowly still-hunting a hardwood ridge that led to a dense stand of white cedar. Deer love to lie in the protection of the cedars, but slipping up on them is next to impossible. I figured if there was a buck in the cedars, a little rattling might bring him out for a look-see.

I positively had the place to myself, so I set up on the ground and

Brad Harris of Lohman Game Calls is an expert white-tailed deer hunter. Over the years, he has used many synthetic rattling systems to dupe mature bucks.

The author used a rattling box to coax this mature Minnesota buck into easy range of his .50-caliber muzzleloader.

took the Lohman clacker out of my fanny pack, laid my muzzleloader on a log in front of me, and started working the plastic paddle against the sides of the box. Within seconds, I spotted deer legs beneath the cedar branches. The skinny legs were pistoning my way in a hurry. By the time I could drop the box and grab my muzzleloader, a buck was skidding to a wide-eyed halt at what I later measured to be seven steps from where I was sitting. At that range, even with the variable scope set on its lowest magnification, all I could see was hair through the lens, so I just let instinct take over. I pointed the muzzle at the buck's chest and touched the trigger.

When the muzzleloader belched, I momentarily lost sight of the buck, but through the haze I could actually see the 250-grain sabot part the hair on his chest. It was the only time I have ever seen a deer literally picked up off of his feet by the impact of a bullet. He died instantly.

When I talked to Harris at the end of the season, I said that despite my reluctance, I found the new rattling device was simple to use, easy to carry and effective for sparring sessions and all-out rattling. I still

Rattling boxes are designed with sound chambers that allow hunters to produce maximum volume. The author's tests show that rattling boxes outperform rattling bags at producing volume, but bags are more convenient and better at producing the tickling sounds of two bucks sparring.

Today, I go back and forth between clackers and rattling bags. Both are light and easy to carry. Both work, but to my ear, rattling bags have a definite edge when it comes to producing more authentic sounds.

---

think it sounds like plastic hitting plastic, but who cares what it sounds like as long as deer like it!

Two years later, Lohman redesigned the call and put two paddles side by side in a slightly larger box and named it "Double Rattle." The addition of the second paddle made the call easier to use and helped it produce more volume. Since then, other call companies have introduced similar rattling devices. While I have not tried them all, my guess is that they all work equally as well.

Today, I go back and forth between clackers and rattling bags. Both are light and easy to carry. Both work, but to my ear, rattling bags have a definite edge when it comes to producing more authentic sounds. In fact, nothing, not even real antlers, can match a rattling bag when it comes to reproducing the tickling sounds of two bucks sparring. On windy days or in open country where I need volume, I go with clackers because their sounds carry farther than those made by bags.

CHAPTER 9

How Loudly Should You Rattle?

The subtitle for this chapter could be "Clancy's Totally Unscientific but Pretty Neat Volume Test." I've always figured that of all of the rattling devices we just covered, the noise of my heavy set of antlers worked the best for reaching out long-distance.

Of course, manufacturers of various rattling devices claimed their contraptions were better at the AT&T gig. To settle the argument for myself, I enlisted the assistance of my teenage daughter Katie. Her initial reaction to my proposal was to roll her eyes back — a nifty trick she learned from her mother — while saying something like, "Get real, Dad!" So I did what any '90s Dad would do. I bribed her. An Oreo Blizzard (a big one, no kid's size) at the Dairy Queen was the price agreed upon. Katie was a reluctant participant, with absolutely zero interest in the outcome, so I can assure you the results are totally unbiased.

We drove to a huge, recently cut hayfield owned by a friend. I gave Katie a Motorola walkie-talkie and laid a similar unit on my pickup's tailgate. Then I had Katie walk 200 yards out into the field with instructions to listen to my rattling and keep walking farther away, stopping to listen every 20 steps or so. As long as she could still hear the rattling, she was to keep walking. When she could no longer hear it she would notify me on the radio.

I would then zap her with a Bushnell Yardage Pro rangefinder. Then I would go to my worksheet and, next to which "instrument" I was using, write down the distance. Like I said, not very scientific, but accurate and honest.

On the day we did the test, the temperature was about 75 degrees, and the skies clear with a 10 to 12 mph breeze out of the north. The wind speed is not my estimate. I verified it with the local airport, which is only a few miles from where we did the test.

This 10-pointer, opposite page, was the first buck to respond to what was going to be a full day of hit-and-run rattling in South Texas.

The most surprising finding of the author's rattling test was that the noise made by synthetic antlers and the real thing carried the same distance.

Consult the chart that follows for the results of our test.

The Katie Clancy Rattling-Volume Test

Instrument	Distance Downwind	Distance Upwind
Real set of rattling antlers:	525 yards	235 yards
Synthetic antlers (Primos)	525 yards	235 yards
Rattling Bag (Knight & Hale)	473 yards	196 yards
Rattling Bag (H.S)	456 yards	173 yards
Lohman Double Rattle	537 yards	241 yards
MAD Power Rattle	556 yards	259 yards

What Did the Test Show?

What did the Katie Clancy test prove? It proved how far away a 13-year-old girl with excellent hearing could hear each of these rattling tools. How does Katie's hearing compare to a whitetail's? Well, because her ears are not quite as big as a deer's (thank God!), there is reason to believe a deer hears far better than Katie, and would hear all of these instruments even farther away.

To me, the most surprising finding was that the noise of synthetic antlers and the real thing carried the same distance. I would have bet the real-bone sound would have carried farther. That tells me Will Primos and his crew of call-makers did their homework when trying to match actual antler density when they designing the synthetic antlers I used in the test.

I'll admit I was disappointed when the real rattling antlers did not come in first place, but that is just the traditionalist in me showing through. Another surprise was how much difference there was between the two rattling bags I tested. I just assumed all rattling bags were created equal, but again I was wrong. What goes inside the bags, wood or synthetic rods and the shape of rods makes a difference. I was also surprised there was not a bigger gap between the Lohman Double

It's not unusual to hear a couple of bucks sparring during the early season. If you can add your own rendition, one or both of the bucks might wander over to check it out. Carrying a rattling bag or a clacker can be good insurance.

Many hunters think sparring is how bucks determine dominance. I believe such matters are decided without antler touching antler, mainly through posturing.

Rattle and the MAD Power Rattle.

I was also surprised at the differences between the upwind and downwind hearing distances. With each tool, the distance at which Katie could hear the rattling was cut at least in half when I was rattling upwind, and that was just in a 10- to 12-mph breeze. No wonder then that every accomplished horn-shaker I know cusses the wind.

If you find any of this helpful, perhaps you can help with the $7.10 I spent treating Miss Katie and the tester me) to lunch at the DQ!

Sparring

Sparring, it has long been believed by many hunters, is how bucks determine dominance. But I don't believe that. These matters are generally sorted out without antler ever touching antler, mainly through posturing. It's like when my buddies and I used to go the beach back in junior high to swim and make fools of ourselves while trying to impress the girls. We tried to pretend we were all pretty tough dudes. But when Kenny Stencel strode onto the beach, all of our posturing was over. Kenny was an all-state wrestler and first-class running back on the football team. His arms were bigger around than my thighs! Kenny was the only guy on the beach who didn't have to stick out his chest to look big and strong for the girls. He was big and strong.

The same thing happens in the whitetail's world. Bucks tend to hang out together in bachelor groups throughout the summer and early autumn. During this lazy period, they begin to sort out who's who according to body size and antler development. A mature 200-pound buck with a sweeping, long-beamed, multi-tined rack does not need to go around whipping all of the other deer to prove his superiority. Like Kenny Stencel, all he has to do is show up.

Sparring isn't about dominance and it has nothing to do with aggression or sex. Those factors kick in with the serious, knock-down, drag-out wars yet to come. When two bucks put their racks together and gently twist their necks and maybe do a little shoving, it's more a sign of recognition than anything. If you and I are old friends and we have

Sometimes all you hear is a brief "click-clickety-click."
If you're not in tune to every sound in the woods, that
sound is easy to miss or dismiss.

not seen each other for a while and we meet one day at the barber shop, what's the first thing we do? Shake hands, right? Deer don't have hands, so they sniff each other instead. (Incidentally, that fact makes me really glad for the human tradition of shaking hands.) And in the case of bucks, they sometimes butt heads a little.

As the rut nears, the sparring matches become more animated. Now bucks dig in and try to knock the other buck off balance, but still, these shoving matches are nothing compared to what's just around the corner.

Sparring Tactics

Imitating a couple of sparring bucks is a tactic worth remembering when hunting during the pre-rut. It's also occasionally effective late in the season after the rut is long over. I typically use sparring sounds to attract bucks I can see and which have already ignored my grunt call or perhaps were unable to hear the grunt call because of winds.

Late one evening, just before quitting time, a buck walked out of a standing cornfield and began crossing a CRP field. He was about 200 yards away from my stand, which was just inside the edge of a wood-lot. I tried to get his attention with the grunt call, but 200 yards is a long way for a deer to hear a grunt, even on a calm day. And on this evening, a cross-wind was blowing about 10 mph. I reached into my fanny pack and grabbed a rattling bag. I rolled the bag between the palms of my hands, causing the dowels inside of the cloth bag to click against each other. The buck heard the sound, stopped and stared in my direction. I was well hidden, so I kept rolling the bag in my hands. The buck stood for maybe 30 seconds and then, with a flick of his tail, turned and marched across the CRP field straight to my stand. When he got closer, I could see that although he was a nice 2½-year-old 8-pointer, he was not what I was looking for so early in the season. The buck milled around my stand a few minutes, searching for the deer he had heard, and then gave up the search and walked off.

Even when rattling is not in my plans for that day, I always carry a rattling bag, a Lohman Double Rattle or a similar device in my fanny

Most days when hunting during the pre-rut or post-rut the author doesn't rattle at all, but there are times when being able to simulate the sound of two bucks sparring has made a difference.

A hunter with good hearing can probably only hear light sparring at 100 yards in timber, and maybe half-again that far in the open. Therefore, when you hear it, you know two bucks are close by.

pack, just in case. Most days when hunting during the pre-rut or post-rut I don't rattle at all, but there are times when being able to simulate the sound of two bucks sparring has made a difference.

I can recall five occasions when I used sparring to attract bucks I could not see but heard sparring. Sometimes all you hear is a brief "click-clickety-click." If you're not in tune to every sound in the woods, that sound is easy to miss or dismiss. But because a hunter with good hearing can probably only hear light sparring at 100 yards in timber, and maybe half-again that far in the open, it pays to listen for the sound. When you hear it, you know two bucks are close by.

A Pre-Rut Tale

In late September one year I was hunting in southeastern Minnesota where the bow season opens at mid-month. With about an hour of shooting light left, I had not yet seen a deer. That's not unusual early in the season, when warm weather greatly suppresses daytime movement.

Suddenly, I heard antlers touching antlers. The contact was brief, no more than a couple of clicks, but I knew what I had heard. I gave a single contact grunt on the tube and waited a few minutes. When nothing showed, I took my Lohman rattle-box and, while holding the box in my left hand, used the palm of my right hand to lightly slap the ceramic paddle against the sides of the box.

The result was a realistic clickety-click-clack. I had just enough time to slip the rattle box into my pocket before a 6-point buck jumped the barbwire fence that circled the pastured timber to my west and slowly walked toward my stand. The little buck walked to the oak in which I sat. When he could not find what he was looking for, he walked up the ridge and disappeared into thick cedars near the ridge's crest.

I waited a few minutes after the 6-pointer had melted from sight and then reached again for the rattling box. I knew the other buck was still in the other patch of timber. Maybe a little more sparring would pique his curiosity. I was just about to begin my sparring sequence when I heard "clickety-click-click-clack." A new round of sparring was coming from the same place I had first heard it. Try as they might, a deer just cannot make that sound by itself, so I knew at least two more bucks were in that woodlot.

Again, I took out the rattle box and did my best to imitate the sound I had just heard. This time an 8-pointer jumped the fence in the same place the 6-pointer had crossed. Like the 6-pointer, the larger buck was coming straight for my stand. This buck was much larger than the 6-pointer, and was probably a year or two older, but the season was still young. With only one buck tag bearing my name, I decided to pass on the 8-pointer, too.

Just then, another buck jumped the fence and started my way. This one, also an 8-pointer, was almost a twin to the second buck. The two bucks milled around my tree a minute or more, and then one of the bucks went up toward the cedars on the ridge. The other buck wandered off in the other direction.

Evidently, the three bucks had still been hanging out together in their summer bachelor group. If they had not decided to do a little head-butting, I would probably never have known they were around. Even though I did not shoot one of them, it was exciting to call them in with the rattling box.

CHAPTER 10

Advanced Rattling Tactics

During peak periods for rattling, my favorite tactic is to cover ground and try to reach as many bucks as possible. The more bucks that hear my rattling antlers during a day of hunting, the better the odds that I'll have multiple encounters. Remember, even on the best properties with balanced doe-to-buck ratios, and even during prime rut time, not every buck that hears rattling is going to respond.

Hit-and-Run Rattling

Hit-and-run rattling won't work if you only have an 80-acre woodlot to hunt. If you're limited in acreage, you're far better off staying put. When I hunt a place with some room to roam, I love using hit-and-run tactics during prime rattling periods. Most of the time I just take off on foot and start covering ground, but I never overlook an opportunity to slip a small boat, canoe or kayak into a stream and let the water carry me from one rattling site to another. Some of the best whitetail habitat in North America is found along such waterways.

Move into the wind or crosswind if you have to. The wind on your back is dangerous because you might spook deer. If you're fanatical about odor control, you might be able to get away with it if you have no other options. During the past five seasons, I've become very odor conscious, and have rattled in numerous bucks from upwind positions. However, given the choice, my preference is to hunt into the wind.

If you're familiar with the country you're hunting, ask yourself where the best places are for a buck to be holed up during the day, then concentrate your efforts on slipping into position for rattling near these areas. These areas are usually near the thickest, nastiest cover around.

When I'm not familiar with the lay of the land, I simply stop every quarter-mile and rattle. I know this random strategy means some of my rattling sessions are probably not conducted within hearing distance of a buck, but I've learned from experience that if I try to move through unfamiliar country looking for prime habitat, I'll invariably move too far between sets and end up spooking deer.

Besides, once the rut is in full swing, you never know where a buck might be. I like to concentrate on heavy cover, but I've had success

Once the rut is in full swing, you never know where a buck might be, so it is a good time to take advantage of hit-and-run rattling. Waterways are a good place to use this tactic.

Never overlook a chance to slip a small boat, canoe or kayak into a stream and let the water carry you from one rattling site to another. Some of the best white-tailed deer habitat in North America is found along such waterways.

rattling in open hardwoods, pastures, CRP fields and wide-open crop-land. I even rattled in one buck that crossed two fairways at the local golf course to investigate the sounds of my rattling.

Once in position, I give a series of tending grunts on my grunt tube and then wait a few minutes. If nothing shows, I start rattling. Some hunters like to rake trees with an antler and beat brush to simulate a buck doing some serious rubbing, but I usually prefer a low-key approach. I start by tickling the tines, slowly at first and then going at it with more gusto by meshing and grinding the antler tines together. Banging the antlers together is unnecessary and might spook a nearby buck. When bucks start to fight, they don't clash together like two bighorn rams on the Dodge truck commercial. I like to start off slow and easy and then build up in volume and intensity.

Combination Calling

Some hunters like to blow on a grunt call while rattling. I use my mouth to imitate the sounds I've heard bucks make when fighting. If you want to rake trees or bushes with the antlers while you rattle, that's fine.

Terry Krahn, a friend of the author, rattled this buck in during late October. The buck was taken in southern Minnesota, a region where many hunters claim rattling doesn't work.

This 9½-year-old buck is the oldest the author has ever taken. The old buck's teeth were almost worn down to the gum line, and its tongue had scars from a winter spent ripping browse. But even this old warrior could not resist the sound of the author's rattling horns.

So is pounding the ground with the antler beams. Some hunters use this tactic to imitate the sound of heavy hoofs seeking firm footing. Make all the racket you want, because I guarantee you, after having observed many full-fledged battles in the wild, you cannot come close to making as much noise as two mature bucks getting it on.

After starting a rattling sequence, keep it up for at least one minute. I know that when I first tried rattling, I felt self-conscious about making noise. After all, I had been taught all of my life to sit still and be quiet when deer hunting, and here I was thrashing and banging antlers together like a crazy man.

It was hard for me to rattle for a minute, so I got in the habit of looking at my watch when I first picked up the antlers and forcing myself to keep up the racket for at least a minute. Sometimes I go on for two or three minutes, especially when hunting semi-open country where I know the sound will carry a long way and a buck might respond from a half-mile or more away.

How far will a buck travel when responding to rattling? I'm not sure

The author enjoys calling foxes and coyotes, and he knows from experience these critters will come to a call from a mile or more away. However, when the calling stops, they often give up. Deer are prone to the same behavior.

about that, but I suspect an interested buck will respond as long as he can hear it. I've rattled in bucks that arrived at the scene with their mouths hanging open as they gasped for air. Those bucks had traveled long distances, and I think that by keeping up the rattling for more than one minute, I encouraged them to complete the trip.

In winter, I enjoy calling foxes and coyotes, and I know from experience these critters will come to a call from a mile or more away. While calling in Western states, where you can see forever, I've observed coyotes come to calls from really long distances. In many cases, the coyotes appeared as tiny specks — no bigger than a pin head — in the distance. As long as I stayed on the call, these long-distance coyotes kept on running toward the call. However, when I stopped calling, they often gave up. Perhaps they figured that the opportunity for an easy meal had been lost.

I can't prove that is the case with deer, but I suspect it is. Bucks coming from a long distance need encouragement to keep on coming, so even though I cannot see them, every time I set up to rattle I picture a heavy-horned, thick-necked buck lumbering steadily toward my position. That mental image keeps me working the horns even after I think I've made enough noise.

That same mental image keeps me alert for the next 10 to 15 minutes as I wait for a buck to arrive. Any experienced rattler will tell you that most of the bucks that come to rattling are there within the first minute or two. In fact, I've had a lot of them show up while I was still working the antlers. However, about 25 percent of the bucks are late. I figure those bucks are worth waiting for.

Try at Least Twice

After waiting 15 minutes without a response, begin another rattling sequence. Wait another 10 minutes. I'll admit that I have seldom lured bucks into range during the second rattling sequence. After giving that advice at seminars, I'm often asked why I don't move after the first sequence. Well, the odds of attracting a buck during the second sequence might be low, but the ones that do respond usually are the big boys.

All of the serious rattling guys I know have reported similar results. It seems that top-end bucks are slow to respond, and they often show up during the second go-around. I'm convinced that if you do a lot of rattling and fail to follow up with a second session, you'll be walking away from big bucks that are taking their time coming to the battle.

Young bucks often show up early because they're so eager to see what

When planning a trip to the Canadian provinces, pack some type of rattling device. Deer densities are low in many parts of Canada, so bucks like this Saskatchewan trophy taken by Mike Wicke look long and hard to find estrous does. These Northern bucks are prime candidates for rattling antlers.

Where visibility is limited, I rattle at least every hour. In open country, where I might be able to see several hundred yards in all directions, I rattle less often and depend on calling to bring deer in close.

all the racket is about. Even some midsize bucks will throw caution to the wind and dash in. But the really big bucks almost always come in slow. I don't know why, but I suspect there are several reasons.

First, the largest, oldest bucks are fairly lazy critters. I compare them to an old black Angus bull lying in the pasture with a bunch of fat, sleek cows. Do you see that bull up and running from cow to cow working himself into a frenzy? Nope, most of the day he just lies on the hill, chewing his cud and taking life easy. Then, when duty calls, he gets up, walks down the hill and does his job. I keep a picture of that old bull in my mind when I get antsy and want to move on before giving the rattling antlers a second try.

Second, I think it takes more effort to convince an old buck that a fight is worth his time. After all, the old boy has seen it all before. He's been in a lot of fights and won some, but he's surely been whipped a few times, too. Maybe the memories of those lost battles make him a little reluctant to answer the call sometimes.

Finally, a mature buck that has been around four or five seasons is not likely to charge blindly into any situation, even when slightly addled by the urge to breed. Instead, he sneaks in, stops often to watch, listen and smell the wind. Mature bucks almost always approach battle scenes downwind of the combatants.

Old bucks are seldom in a hurry. You should not be, either, if you want to get a look at them.

Rattling From a Stand

I'm often asked, "How often should I rattle when hunting from a stand?" I always feel like a politician when I answer with my standard, "Well, that depends on the situation."

But the truth is, my rattling frequency when hunting from a stand depends on the situation. During the prime time for rattling — the two-week period leading up to the breeding phase of the rut and the breeding phase itself — I pick up the antlers based on these factors:

✓ Is the area a prime candidate for rattling? If the answer is "yes," I

There are days when sitting still and not making noise seems like the right thing to do. Then there are days when I can't stand to sit, so I rattle up a storm. I have learned to follow my instincts.

rattle the bones for a minute or two at least once an hour. If I'm hunting an area where I know the herd structure is not in my favor, I might rattle only a couple times the entire day.

✓ Is it calm or breezy? Wind has a big influence on how much I rattle when I'm on stand. If it's calm, I rely heavily on calling because my calls can be heard for long distances. I'll commonly use a series of tending grunts with a few estrous-doe bleats thrown in three to four times an hour. If it's breezy, I'll hammer the antlers more often because I know deer can hear them at greater distances than they can hear grunt calls.

✓ Is the cover thick or semi-open? Where visibility is limited, I rattle at least every hour. In open country, where I might be able to see several hundred yards in all directions, I rattle less often and depend on calling to bring deer in close.

✓ Will I hunt with or without a decoy? If I'm using a decoy, I rattle more often than when I'm hunting without a decoy because I want to create maximum opportunities for a buck to see my decoy.

✓ By rattling, do I run the risk of calling in other hunters? Don't laugh, but I've called in several sheepish hunters over the years. If I suspect other hunters are within hearing distance, I rattle sparingly. The last thing I want is another hunter putting the sneak on my position, although I admit it's fun to watch!

✓ What are the deer doing? I rattle more often when deer are active and less when I'm not seeing much movement. Bucks are more inclined to come to rattling when they are up and moving. They are less likely to respond when they're bedded. By the way, this is the reason why rattling success is nearly always higher in the mornings than in the afternoons.

✓ What kind of mood am I in? There are days when sitting still and not making noise seems like the right thing to do. Then there are days when I can't stand to sit, so I rattle up a storm. I have learned to follow my instincts.

Toss Those Horns
When I'm hunting from a tree stand and using a set of rattling antlers,

I tie my pull-up rope to the cord that connects the two rattling antlers. I do this for a couple of reasons.

The first deer I ever rattled in, a decent Minnesota buck, came charging hard out of a standing cornfield and burst for my tree stand site before I was halfway through my first rattling session. When I tried to hang the antlers from a limb stub and grab my bow, the antlers clunked together. The buck looked up, evidently thinking it was a tad strange that the bucks he had heard were now fighting 20 feet up a cottonwood tree. He immediately made a mad dash for the cornfield. I'm not a real quick learner, so it wasn't until the same thing happened again the next season that I started tying my rattling antlers to my pull-up rope.

I soon learned that tossing my antlers to the ground is a great tactic. In fact, I still use it today. When I'm rattling and a buck suddenly appears, I toss the antlers to the ground and grab my gun or bow. The commotion of the antlers hitting the ground doesn't spook deer. In fact, I think it helps. The clatter of the antlers hitting the ground usually zeroes a buck's attention on that area. Just be sure that the pull-up rope is long enough so that the antlers hit the ground. Oh yes, and be sure to tie the other end of the rope to a branch. Even when you're alone, it's embarrassing to have to climb down from your stand to retrieve your rope and antlers!

On three occasions, I watched as bucks hung up out of range after I tossed my antlers to the ground. In desperation, I jerked on the pull-up rope so the antlers clacked against each other on the ground. In all three instances, that ruse did the trick and the bucks closed the distance. Because deer are pretty good at pinpointing the source of a sound, I don't like to rattle from my tree stand when a buck is close. But with the antlers at ground level, a buck will not scan the treetops for trouble.

When bucks don't come within shooting range, or when I pass up a buck, I wait until the deer leaves the area before retrieving the antlers. This is a neat trick that has worked well for me over the years, and it will also work for you.

CHAPTER 11

Is Decoying Really for You?

I was talking at the Shooting, Hunting and Outdoors Trade Show one year with the owner of a major decoy manufacturing company. When we ran out of stories to share, Jim turned serious and said: "You know, Clancy, I don't understand why every deer hunter in America isn't using a decoy. I mean, look at the tales you and I have just shared about just one season of hunting with a decoy. Wouldn't you think every hunter out there would be beating down the doors trying to buy a decoy?"

"Well, Jim," I said, "you know I'm a big believer in decoys and use them a lot. But I'm the first to admit that decoys are not for everyone."

Jim looked like I had just delivered a hard right to his gut. Decoy manufacturers don't want to hear stuff like that. They prefer big numbers. But the reality, as I see it, is that only a small percentage of the 12 million deer hunters in North America will ever hunt over a decoy.

I can think of several reasons for this. The big reason is that in most situations, using a decoy during a firearms season falls somewhere between suicidal and highly risky. Unless someone is reading this book to you, I probably don't have to explain why. Yes, using a decoy during a firearms season in unique situations is not likely to draw "friendly fire," but such instances are most unusual across North American. I usually don't want any part of it, because I can tell you from experience that friendly fire is no less frightening or lethal than hostile fire.

Some Unique Situations

Still, I've done it when the situation is unique. For instance, a decoy can be safely positioned on a South Texas sendero while the hunter occupies a shooting tower. But those situations are usually unique to ranches where hunting is limited to a few deep-pocketed guests each week, and trespassers are likely to simply disappear.

Other situations that can be safe are the vast, private ranches of the West. The Northern forests of Ontario, Manitoba, Saskatchewan and Alberta are other places where I would use a decoy during a gun season. In fact, a decoy setup near a bait station — which is the most common way of hunting in Saskatchewan — is a great way to lure old bucks into the open where you can get a whack at them. Anyone who has hunted

The average bow-hunter is convinced rattling only works in Texas. He might also dump some doe pee on his boots, but he really doesn't believe it does much good. The average bow-hunter probably won't buy a decoy.

The average bow-hunter buys a bow and some arrows because his buddies are into bow-hunting. He gets out a few times each season, enjoys the solitude, and watches the birds and all that stuff.

Saskatchewan can verify the biggest bucks have a nasty habit of just cruising by bait stations looking for does, but never showing themselves. A decoy will give them what they're looking for. There have also been times when I have hunted special muzzleloader-only seasons in which hunting pressure was non-existent and using a decoy was safe. Or you might be fortunate enough to hunt on your own land. But even then, you must make sure that any other friends or relatives hunting the land know you're using a decoy.

In all of the above cases, I wouldn't hesitate to use a decoy. But those are very special situations. In most cases, I discourage the use of decoys during any part of a firearms deer season.

So that leaves decoying as the main domain of bow-hunters. OK, we still have several million bow-hunters to work with. If half of them bought a deer decoy, Jim-the-decoy-maker would be one rich, happy camper. Jim figures reaching half the continent's bow-hunters should be a cinch. That's because Jim, like a lot of archery-related manufacturers, might have a faulty perception of today's bow-hunter.

Who Wants a Decoy?

In Jim's mind, when the word "bow-hunter" is spoken, he pictures a person totally dedicated to bow-hunting deer. He sees someone who is fanatical about choosing the best equipment and using it properly. This bow-hunter scouts year-around, knows the country he hunts better than his own living room, haunts every 3-D shoot within 200 miles of home, and is paranoid about human odor. He also owns 16 grunt calls, four sets of rattling antlers, and stocks his refrigerator in the garage with countless bottles of deer scent. This bow-hunter saves most of his vacation for archery deer season (the rut, naturally) and spends every minute he can during bow season perched in his stand, regardless of weather, and loves every second of it.

Such a bow-hunter is a prime candidate for a decoy.

But is that guy your "average" bow-hunter, the guy who makes up the bulk of bow-hunting's vast numbers? I don't think so. Your average bow-

Only a small percentage of the 12 million deer hunters in North America will ever hunt over a decoy. They probably think it's too much of a bother.

hunter bought a bow and some arrows because his buddies are into bow-hunting. He gets out a few times each season, enjoys the solitude, and watches the birds and all that stuff.

Once in awhile he gets a shot at a deer, and every few years he actually gets one. But most of the time he depends on the gun season to put venison in the freezer.

The average bow-hunter has a grunt call. Somewhere. He used it once, but it didn't seem to fool any deer, so he put it somewhere. The average bow-hunter is convinced rattling only works in Texas. Sometimes he dumps some doe pee on his boots when he walks into the woods, but he really doesn't believe it does much good. He does urinate in scrapes, though, because his buddy Joe said this can really turn bucks on.

When it comes to odor control, the average bow-hunter figures you can't do anything but keep the wind in your favor. He also believes Scent-Lok is some kind of child-proof cap for Tink's 69!

I could go on, but you probably get the drift. The average bow-hunting guy ain't buying no decoy!

A big reason many hunters won't ever use a decoy is that using one during a firearms season falls somewhere between suicidal and highly risky.

You're Not the Average Guy

You're probably wondering how I dare say all these terrible things about the average bow-hunter. Aren't I worried about offending those millions of "average" bow-hunters who will read this book?

Ah ha! There's the kicker. The average bow-hunter I just described will not plunk down $19.95 for this book. And even if you give him your copy to read, he won't get this far. The chapters on calling and rattling have already convinced him the whole book is full of more of that hocus-pocus stuff that doesn't work where he hunts.

So that leaves only you and others like you. You're the serious white-tailed deer hunters. You are Jim-the-decoy-maker's potential customers. So should each of you rush out and buy a decoy? Probably not.

Here's why: A person might be a serious hunter, but that doesn't mean he's strictly a big-buck hunter or even a buck hunter. Many excellent, deeply serious archers are meat hunters, and I use that term with respect. I know bow-hunters of the meat-hunter variety who are every bit as good at the game as guys who focus all of their attention on the largest bucks. Meat hunters are tickled to take whatever deer presents them an opportu-

Hunters who use decoys tend to be on the analytical side. You might even call them suspicious. Most are already excellent deer hunters, but despite their success, they're always looking to improve.

nity for a good shot. Because does, and especially does with fawns, are often skittish around decoys, especially during the rut, using a decoy could cost these hunters their best shooting opportunities.

Other excellent bow-hunters are what I call the "Au Natural" variety. These hunters work hard not to disturb the area they're hunting. That means no scents, no calling and no rattling. Just slip in when the wind is right and wait them out. No decoys for this bunch!

Then there are "gear-weary" bow-hunters. This group is tired of all of the gizmos and gadgets available to today's archer. They desperately try to stay lean and mean in the equipment category. I can't argue with this group, either. On many days I've labored up a steep ridge to my stand with a bulging backpack full of "essentials" strapped to my shoulders and a decoy under one arm. At such times I longed for those innocent days of my youth when all I owned was four arrows and a Herter's solid glass recurve bow that was stamped 55#. (Of course, that bow pulled like 100 pounds, but that's another story.)

My point is this: Who really thinks these equipment-conscience folks are going to lug around a decoy?

So, Who Uses a Decoy?

Lots of hunters read an article about decoying deer or see a video in which a decoy is used, and then rush out and buy a decoy. But after lugging the decoy through the woods, using it at the wrong time and place, and getting bad results, the bow-hunter tosses his decoy atop all the other things that were supposed to be the magic pill.

Even though such guys keep decoy manufacturers in business, they don't use them.

Let's make sure we all understand something vital: A decoy won't make up for sloppy or lazy hunting tactics. A decoy is also no substitute for scouting. As deadly as decoys can be, they're worthless if your hunting technique stinks or you're hunting in the wrong place at the wrong time.

The hunters I know who really use decoys tend to be on the analytical side. You might even call them suspicious. Most are already excellent deer hunters, but despite their success, they're always looking to improve. When they read about something new, like decoys, they don't rush to the phone, pull out their Visa card and place an order with Cabela's. Instead, they use their experience to answer their own questions:

✓ Does it make sense that deer would be attracted to a decoy?

All a buck wants is visual confirmation of what it has heard. A decoy provides that all-important deal-closer.

In many cases, hunters have experimented with crude homemade decoys before plunking down the cash for a commercial model.

✓ Does it make sense that using a decoy will focus the deer's attention on the decoy, making it easier for me to draw my bow undetected?

✓ Does it make sense that using a decoy will help me position the deer for the perfect angle for the shot?

✓ Does it make sense that a decoy will provide the visual confirmation some bucks seek after responding to antlers or calls?

In many cases, these hunters have experimented with crude homemade decoys before plunking down the cash for a commercial model. Bruce Hudalla is a good example. Hudalla runs a marketing company that handles several top manufacturers of archery equipment. He also just happens to be one of the better bow-hunters I've ever met. Hudalla loves to rattle in big bucks, but like many hunters, his experience with the biggest bucks was that they rarely rushed in blindly to the horns.

Instead, the big boys commonly hang up out of bow range to survey the situation. They're smart enough to know that if they can hear those bucks fighting, they ought to be able to at least get a glimpse of them.

If they don't, more often than not the jig is up.

The Hudalla Goblin Caper

As a result, Hudalla made a "little goblin." He took a baseball-sized rock and draped it with a white cloth about the size of a dishtowel. By tying the cloth off under the rock, he was able to make the rock form the goblin's head and the rest of the cloth form a skirt. Then he took an old level-wind casting reel, spooled it with tough monofilament line, and attached the reel to a short, stout ice-fishing rod.

As Hudalla told me about his little goblin, I detected a hint of embarrassment in his voice as he recalled how it felt to climb into his tree stand with a rod, reel, and homemade ghost with a rock head! I assured him I knew exactly how he felt. After all, I'm the guy who tried to rattle in bucks with my dog's locator bell! I also assured Hudalla that he had nothing to be embarrassed about. Nearly every deer hunter who stands a notch or two above the masses has experimented with some off-the-wall schemes in their never-ending quest to fool Mr. Whitetail.

Once in his stand, Hudalla would pick out a tree branch in front of his

Before deciding whether to use a decoy, ask yourself if you're willing to go through the hassle of lugging a decoy to your stand.

blind and make a cast over the branch. He would then lower the little goblin until it was four or five feet off the ground, engage the reel, and stick the stubby rod into a crotch of the tree within easy reach.

"That little goblin worked better than I ever expected," Hudalla told me. "The second or third time I used it, I rattled in a nice buck, but he just stood back there in the brush like the big ones so often do. I could see one side of his rack and his eye, and that was it. I reached over, grabbed the fish line and made that little goblin dance up and down. The buck charged in so fast I barely had time to drop the fish line and grab my bow. All a buck wants is visual confirmation of what it has heard. Until I started using a decoy, that little goblin provided that visual confirmation."

Check Your Questions

Check those first questions again. If the answer to them is yes, then ask some more questions.

✓ Am I willing to go through the hassle of lugging a decoy into the woods?

✓ Does a decoy fit into my style of hunting?

✓ Is a decoy going to be safe where I hunt?

✓ Will a decoy draw unwanted attention to my stand locations?

✓ Am I convinced enough to give decoying a fair try and not give up after one or two hunts when nothing responds to my decoys?

✓ Am I willing to accept the fact that no matter how careful I am when placing the decoy and controlling scent on it, occasionally a deer will spook from the decoy?

If the answer to all these questions is still yes, then you're ready to try hunting over a decoy. Welcome aboard, you're going to have some fun!

CHAPTER 12

Choosing the Right Decoy for You

OK, so you've made up your mind. This is the year you're going to give decoying deer a try. Good for you. You're going to have a blast! Now let's talk about the nuts and bolts of using decoys in the field.

Hunting over a decoy is a lot of fun. Getting the decoy to where you want to hunt usually is not. In fact, I think the No. 1 reason more hunters don't hunt with a decoy is that they don't want to be bothered hauling the darned things.

Hauling the Darned Things

To make the job easier, here are some of the things that have worked for me.

Whenever possible, use a vehicle. Except in wilderness settings, deer are accustomed to vehicle traffic. A pickup, ATV or tractor will not cause deer to turn tail and flee the county. What I like to do is use a vehicle to haul my decoy or decoys into or near the stand before my hunt. Let's say, for instance, that I plan to hunt a hilltop stand at the far corner of a big harvested cornfield in the morning. To reach this stand, I need to park at the bottom of the hill, walk up a woodland path the farmer uses to get his machinery to the field, cross the long field, and climb into my stand. Instead of lugging my decoy all of the way to the stand that morning, I will drive near my stand the afternoon before my hunt and stash the decoy in a deadfall or ditch somewhere near the stand.

If I were hunting the same stand in the afternoon, I would simply drive to the stand, leave the vehicle running, unload the decoy, and drive back down the hill to park the vehicle.

Most deer are more accepting of vehicles and motorized machinery than they are of walking, standing or sitting humans. Deer that have not had bad experiences with vehicles (such as poaching and road-hunting) usually just stay bedded or stand their ground and watch the vehicle pass by. As long as the vehicle doesn't stop, deer don't even take evasive action.

Sometimes it's best to have someone drive you and your decoy to the stand site. This might sound lazy, but it's not. In most areas of the country, you'll spook far fewer deer by having someone drive you into the stand site than by walking to it.

Sometimes I get real lucky and have someone available to drive me and the decoy to the stand site. This might sound like I'm being lazy, but I'm not. In most areas of the country today, I know I'll spook far fewer deer by having someone drive me into the stand site, quickly drop me off and then leave than I will by walking into my stand.

But remember, the key word here is "quickly." When I get dropped off at a stand, it doesn't take me 10 seconds to get out of the vehicle, grab my gear (decoy included), and send the vehicle on its way. This is no time to be slamming doors or joking and talking with the driver. Just slip out quietly, grab your gear and tell the driver to get lost.

Tips for Easier Carrying

Of course, I cannot always use a vehicle to transport my decoy. In fact, most of the time I carry my decoy to the stand. When using a silhouette decoy, this isn't much of a burden. But when using a full-body decoy,

By drilling a few holes in the belly of a full-bodied decoy, you can use a rope as a handy carrying sling. When setting up the decoy, simply tuck the rope into the belly.

just getting the decoy to the stand can be a real sweat-maker. To make the job easier, try these tips. Drill a couple of holes in the belly of your decoy if it's a Carry-Lite or Flambeau, and then run a rope through the holes to make a carrying strap. I like enough rope so that when I loop the rope over my shoulder, the decoy rides at hip level. When you set up the decoy you can stuff the rope inside its cavity, but don't worry if the rope dangles from the decoy's belly. Deer won't notice it.

I usually leave the head attached to the decoy, but remove the ears and antlers and place them in the decoy's body cavity. If you don't, you'll probably end up hunting with a one-antlered or one-eared decoy, because both tend to fall out easily. If you lose an ear or antler, don't panic. I've lost a bunch of antlers and ears, but the deer don't seem to care. It just looks kind of goofy.

If I'm going to be walking through brush or timber, I also remove the legs. If I don't, they'll catch on limbs and brush. However, if I'm mostly

For easier carrying, the author takes the ears and antlers off the decoy during transportation. To avoid getting tangled up, he also removes the legs when going through brush or woods.

hiking across fields, I leave the legs intact.

When I must lug a decoy a long distance or when I have a lot of stuff to carry — like maybe heavy winter clothing for late-season hunting — I'll use a backpack or pack frame to carry my decoy. Cabela's and other outlets carry a dandy backpack with a folding platform that's designed for carrying a sleeping bag or light tent. The folding platform carries the decoy nicely. I also like these packs because they can double as a back support when I lean back against the pack to glass fields before I cross.

Of course, if you don't have far to go, you can just throw the decoy over your shoulder and take off.

The Setup

It's easy to properly position the decoy if you remember these three key points.

✓ The decoy must be within shooting range. I know that sounds elementary, but you would be surprised how many hunters place the decoy at or beyond their maximum effective range. A friend once borrowed one of my decoys and went hunting. When he brought it back a few days later, I asked how the decoy had worked.

"The decoy worked all right," he said. "I had a lone doe and two different bucks come into it, but they just wouldn't come close enough for me to get a shot."

Upon further questioning, my friend divulged he had set up the decoy in the middle of an alfalfa field. He figured the decoy was a good 200 yards from his stand. Now that is a long shot with bow and arrow!

✓ Place the decoy where it will be visible at a distance to approaching deer. The farther they can see it the better. A little knoll or hill is better than a dip or low spot in a field because the decoy will be visible from a longer distance. On logging roads, I look for straight stretches where my decoy has maximum visibility.

If deer have to be right on top of the decoy before they can see it, not only will the decoy attract fewer deer, but approaching deer will be shocked when rounding a bend and coming face to face with a decoy. Such a scare will often spook them.

✓ The wind should be blowing from your decoy to your stand or, at least, be a crosswind. If you use a buck decoy, face the decoy at your stand or quartering toward the stand. A buck will nearly always come around to the head of a buck decoy. This will position the buck perfectly for a good shot. When using a doe, do the opposite. You want to be look-ing at a doe decoy's rear end. This is where the buck will do his sniffing.

A proper setup is important if a decoy is to perform as it should. Make sure the decoy is visible, within preferred shooting distance of your stand, and upwind or at least crosswind from your stand.

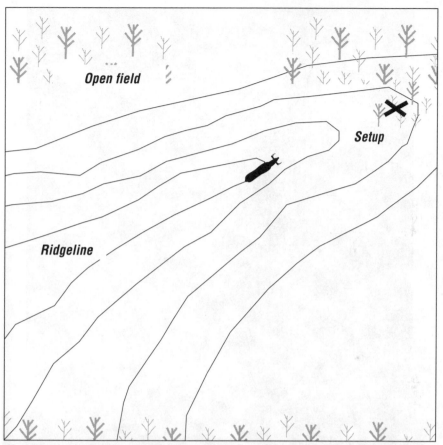

Here is an example of a perfect stand location for using a decoy. In this diagram, the field is surrounded by timber. There is a hill or a ridge down the center of the field. A point of timber connects with this ridge. A decoy placed on the ridge is visible from nearly anywhere in the field or the timber edge.

One Last Thought

There is some persistent misinformation floating around that says hunters should never place the decoy facing their stand because deer tend to look where other deer are looking. The critics say positioning the decoy head-on will increase the odds that a deer coming to the decoy will spot you in the stand.

In my experience, this is simply not true. When a deer comes into a decoy, its focus is on the decoy more than anything else. That is one of the advantages of using a decoy.

CHAPTER 13

When to Use Decoys

With a few exceptions — which we'll cover later in this chapter — the best time to use a decoy is anytime bucks are focusing on sex. In regions with a short, well-defined breeding period, the best time to use a decoy is the two weeks leading up to the onset of serious breeding activity. This is when intense scraping occurs. Decoying will continue to work right on through the breeding period and last until about a week after the frenzy of the breeding period subsides. In all, this is a five- to six-week period.

In the Deep South and Southeastern states, the rut varies greatly by region, which makes it difficult for me to make broad statements about the timing of the rut. Of course, there are a few exceptions, such as parts of Georgia and Alabama. Some deer in those states are descendants of deer live-trapped in Wisconsin and released in these areas in the 1950s. It appears these descendants have maintained the November rut tendencies of their Northern ancestors. However, in many regions, the Southern rut is scattered over a prolonged time period. This doesn't mean decoys don't work in the South, because they do. But don't expect the kind of action that can happen in many Northern areas where the annual rut is intense and short-lived.

Decoys and the Rut's Scraping Phase

To narrow it down even further, my favorite time to use decoys — and the period in which I've had the best response to decoys — is during the scraping phase of the rut. When I start finding serious breeding scrapes, I know it's time to start hunting over a decoy. Decoy action gets better with each passing day of the scraping phase. The last few days of scraping activity — just before bucks mostly abandon scrapes and take up the irresistible scent of the year's first hot does — are the best days of all.

In most of North America, the author discourages hunters from using decoys during a firearms season. This picture, opposite page, was taken during a 1992 muzzleloading season in the remote forests of Saskatchewan. Even where the law doesn't require blaze orange, the author recommends its use during any firearms season.

When the author goes through the bother of lugging a decoy to a stand, it's because he thinks it will help him attract a big buck. Unlike a doe decoy, a buck decoy is more likely to attract aggressive bucks, not just any ol' deer.

Most of the time I rely on one decoy to work its magic. I prefer to use antlers on the decoy, which, of course, imitates a buck. The reason for this is that sometimes a doe decoy attracts too many deer. Too many deer? I know you're thinking that Clancy's really lost it this time.

Let me explain what I mean by "too many deer." When I'm hunting over a decoy, I'm hunting for a buck. Don't get me wrong, I have nothing against shooting does. I've shot a lot of them. My kids grew up on venison, much of it from fat does and tender fawns. But when I go through the bother of lugging a decoy around, it's because I think it will help me attract a big buck. Sure, bucks are attracted to doe decoys, but all deer can be attracted to a doe decoy.

What's wrong with having a couple of does and fawns hanging around the decoy? Absolutely nothing, if they would only behave

Doe decoys will attract some bucks, but they will also pull in does and fawns. The author prefers not to have some cautious does around his stand when bucks are in the area. A wise doe usually gets suspicious and raises a fuss.

themselves! In fact, having a live decoy or two in front of the stand would be great. The problem is that invariably an old doe gets suspicious of the decoy. You know how those mature does are. They're just naturally suspicious of everything. It goes with the territory when you raise young ones, I guess. Although a doe might accept the decoy for a while, most of the time she starts acting up, getting nervous, stalking around the decoy. She might even stamp her forehoof in an attempt to get the decoy to move. Then she'll start to blow and snort.

This kind of behavior is not conducive to bringing in a buck. If a buck happens along while this is going on, he'll know something is wrong. Even that would not be so bad if the doe would just do her thing and leave, but she doesn't. I've had does carry on like this for over a half-hour. Does and fawns are not as attracted to a buck decoy. In fact, in many cases, does — especially as the rut nears — go out of

Some very good hunters who enjoy hunting over a decoy during the scraping phase will put their decoys away once the actual breeding period begins. Is this a mistake? That mostly depends on the doe-to-buck ratio in the area they are hunting.

Some bucks walk around with a chip on their shoulder. During the rut, they're always looking for a fight. A buck decoy gives these bullies an easy target. In turn, this trait makes bucks an easier target for hunters!

their way to avoid contact with bucks, which are making pests of themselves.

As long as we're discussing buck vs. doe decoys, I'll tell you the other reasons I prefer a buck decoy most of the time.

✔ When I use a decoy, I also rely heavily on rattling, calling or both. A buck coming into the sound of rattling antlers or a tending grunt expects to see a buck.

✔ A buck decoy might invoke an aggressive territorial response from a buck, especially if it's the area's dominant buck. A doe decoy will not.

✔ Some bucks, like some people, walk around with a chip on their shoulder. During the rut, these bucks are always looking for a fight. A buck decoy gives these bullies an easy target. In turn, their personality makes them an easy target for me!

With that said, there is one short period during the rut when I prefer a doe decoy. Right at the end of the scraping period, bucks enter what outdoor writer Charles J. Alsheimer dubbed the "chase phase." The chase phase happens during the three or four days right before breeding begins. During this short period, bucks are so sexually charged that you'll see them chasing every doe they lay eyes on. They seem to be hoping against hope that one of them will actually stand still long enough to give them a chance. When I see bucks engaged in this type of activity, the antlers come off my decoy.

Decoys During the Rut's Breeding Phase

I know some good hunters who report solid action with decoys during the scraping phase, but then put their decoys away for the season once actual breeding begins. Is that a mistake? That depends on the doe-to-buck ratio in the area they're hunting.

That term, "doe-to-buck ratio" is commonly heard wherever deer hunters gather. The comments usually go something like this: "Man, our doe-to-buck ratio is so out of whack it's a wonder we ever get a buck. I saw 25 does today and only two small bucks. The DNR is so

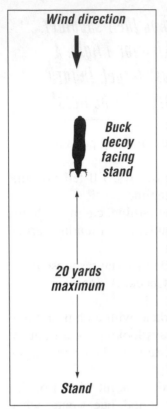

Wind direction

Buck decoy facing stand

20 yards maximum

Stand

Here's how the author sets up when he's hunting over a single buck decoy. To improve his odds, he places the decoy no farther than 20 yards from his stand. The decoy faces the stand, because most bucks will approach a buck decoy from the front, which puts them in bow range.

far off on their doe-to-buck figures that it ain't even funny."

I have to chuckle when I hear such outrageous claims. What that hunter really saw was not 25 does, but rather 25 antlerless deer. A more accurate way to describe sighting is to compare the number of adult does and bucks in the population. I don't count fawns in this equation, but typically the percentage of male and female fawns is nearly 50-50. But because many hunters count every antlerless deer as a doe, the doe-to-buck ratio is often at least three times as high as the number referenced by an agency biologist.

The bottom line is that the higher the doe-to-buck ratio, the less likely you are to have bucks respond to your decoy, or to rattling or calling, during the breeding phase of the rut. When the doe-to-buck ratio is high, say 4-1 or higher, all available breeding-age bucks are incredibly busy during the rut's breeding period. Rare is the buck that will leave an estrous doe to check out a decoy. Yes, it happens, but then, so do total eclipses of the moon.

Long-Term Impacts

I should also point out that not only will a high doe-to-buck ratio make decoying mostly futile during the rut's breeding phase, but it will also dampen a buck's enthusiasm for responding to decoys, rattling or

In scenarios with an artificially high doe-to-buck ratio, a lack of competition means bucks have little or no motivation to be active in daylight.

When using a lone doe decoy in the standing position, this is the best arrangement. Position the doe facing directly away from your stand. Most bucks coming in to check out a doe decoy will approach from the rear.

Wind direction

Doe decoy facing away

20 yards maximum

Stand

calling throughout the season. This occurs because competition between bucks induces them to make lots of rubs and scrapes, and to spend their daylight hours interacting in rut-related activities.

In areas where hunters hammer the bucks and lay off the does to create artificially high doe-to-buck ratios, there is little serious competition between bucks. As a result, they have little motivation to be active in daylight. I also believe more rut-related activities are conducted at night in herds with high doe-to-buck ratios. Naturally, if bucks are not inspired to move during shooting hours, there is little likelihood of a buck encountering your decoy.

Another factor to consider is the impact of the age structure in the buck population. This will have a big bearing on how much success you'll have hunting over a decoy. A well-tuned herd will not only have a reasonable doe-to-buck ratio, but also bucks of several age classes, not just yearlings carrying their first racks. In well-managed herds, bucks 3 years and older will compete for most of the breeding fun. These bucks will also be active making rubs and scrapes.

Because competition between bucks is inherent in that scenario, bucks will be forced to engage in these ancient rituals day and night. This bodes well for the hunter.

Is such a herd living where you hunt? In places where 75 percent to even 90 percent of the bucks are killed each season, you don't have to be a population-demographics expert to realize only a tiny percentage of the buck population will consist of bucks 3 years or older.

Which brings us full circle to the original question about using decoys during the rut's breeding phase. If the doe-to-buck ratio in your hunting area is low enough, some bucks will be without does during the peak of the breeding frenzy. As a result, your decoy will likely see

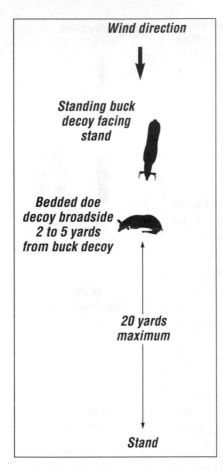

Wind direction

Standing buck decoy facing stand

Bedded doe decoy broadside 2 to 5 yards from buck decoy

20 yards maximum

Stand

During the rut, a doe will often bed down and rest while a buck "stands guard" nearby. The buck stays close to make sure the doe doesn't leave before he can breed her. When trying to mimic this scene with decoys, the author places his buck decoy two to five yards from the doe decoy. He places the doe decoy no more than 20 yards from his tree stand.

some action. And if you're lucky enough to be hunting an area where the sex ratio is reasonable and maybe 25 percent of the bucks are 3 years or older, you should be hunting over a decoy.

Even if most of the mature bucks are busy with hot does, your decoy will get interest from the younger bucks. In a herd with the right dynamics, bucks 2½ years old and younger rarely get to join the festivities.

Post-Rut Decoying

I'm not going to sugar-coat anything about decoying during the post-rut. The truth is, the post-rut is a darned tough time to kill a good buck, regardless of which method you try. Bucks are physically worn out after weeks of acting like fools. In addition, their testosterone levels have dropped at least to the floor, and the breeding urge is fading.

Now they're seeking food and rest. They spend most of the night eating and most of the day napping and chewing their cud. That's not a rosy picture for hunting, but it's accurate. This is what you're up against in the post-rut. Does that mean you should stay home, and find a dry place to store your decoy for the winter? Absolutely not. Here's why:

The onset of the rut's breeding phase, especially in areas with a short, well-defined rut, is often described as "throwing the light switch." One day not much is happening, and the next day bucks are

Hunting over two standing decoys requires a different setup. Place the buck decoy quartering toward your stand, and position the doe decoy quartering away. The maximum distance between the buck's head and the doe's rump is 20 yards from your tree stand.

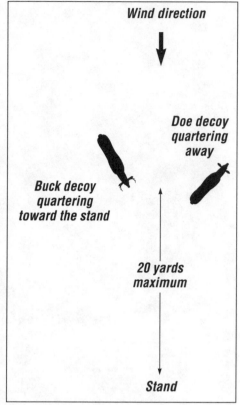

Wind direction

Doe decoy quartering away

Buck decoy quartering toward the stand

20 yards maximum

Stand

running does everywhere. Although it's common for the breeding period to start with a bang, it tapers off more gradually. After two or three days of hot and heavy action, buck movement tends to level off and gradually decline.

The breeding period is generally considered to be that time during which about 70 percent of the does are bred. Usually, this period lasts a week to 10 days. Therefore, if 70 percent of the does are bred during the peak of the rut, that still leaves 30 percent unbred. A few of these does will cycle during or before the "official" start of the breeding phase. Some does might have been bred, but did not conceive. Or they might not have had the opportunity to breed during their estrous cycle. These does will have another estrous period in about 28 days.

There are also does that come into estrus late in the breeding phase and into the first week or so of the post-rut. While the bucks are willing and able to be of service as time goes on, they're not as gung-ho about the procreation thing as they were a few weeks before.

Using Multiple Sets

When I use a decoy during this period, I usually use a buck and a doe. I want to give the impression of a buck standing over a doe in heat. Sometimes I use a standing buck and a standing doe, but usually — because it's easier to carry — I use a lightweight Feather-Flex foam bedded doe, and a full-body plastic buck standing over her. This is a

When using more than one full-body decoy, it's nearly impossible to get them into position near your stand without the help of another hunter. If a friend isn't available, use a vehicle to carry the decoys to your stand site, drop them off, and then finish setting them up just before climbing into your stand.

deadly combination where the ground cover is not so high or thick that it obscures the bedded doe.

By the way, this same setup will also work well during the peak of the rut, but I'm not convinced it will pull anymore bucks at that time than a single decoy.

When I hunt over my decoys during the first week or two of the post-rut, I don't anticipate the kind of action I've enjoyed during the scraping or breeding phases. Hunting over a decoy in the post-rut is not a numbers game, but it might give you your best chance of bringing in a bruiser.

*Early in the post-rut, the rutting fires still smolder
in the buck's belly. But once the season gets
well into the post-rut, bucks spend almost all
of their time eating and resting.*

Like most hunters, I enjoy reading about other hunters' successes. Many magazines run articles about hunters who have killed exceptional bucks during the previous season. In reading these articles, I've noticed that a fairly high percentage of these big bucks were taken during the post-rut. Because so much emphasis is placed on hunting the rut for big bucks, we sometimes overlook other opportunities. This appears to be the case with the post-rut, and more specifically, the first week or two of the post-rut.

In most cases, the herd's largest bucks are responsible for the bulk of the breeding. These bucks exploit every possible breeding opportunity, and they do not give up easily.

Once the bulk of the does have been bred, the most active breeder bucks stay on the move looking for the few receptive does remaining. These bucks aren't content to rest on their laurels.

Is the Post-Rut Your Ace in the Hole?

Because few does are entering estrus during this period, the bucks cover a lot of ground to find that rare willing female. Your ace in the hole for hunting with a decoy could be the first week or two of the post-rut.

Why? Let's reason this out: During the rut's peak, the herd's largest bucks are nearly always with an estrous doe. The odds of such a buck coming to rattling, calling or a decoy are slim. But now you have that same buck out cruising for one last chance. Do you think he won't want to check out your decoys?

But remember, we're talking about early in the post-rut, while rutting fires still smolder in the buck's belly. Once the season gets well into the post-rut, bucks spend almost all of their time eating and resting. For the most part, they couldn't care less about rattling antlers, decoys or grunt calls.

CHAPTER 14

Doctoring Your Decoys

I bought my first car, a 1947 Mercury coupe, in 1966, the same year I grad-
uated from high school. That Merc was a thing of beauty: coal black,
mohair interior and an 85 horsepower flathead 8-cylinder engine. As a hunting car, the Merc was just fine as is, but when it came to impressing the girls
— which was secondary to hunting, but still important — the Merc needed a
little something extra.

I dropped a week's pay on a set of baby moon hubcaps, chrome wheel
rings and a Walker glass-pack muffler. Then my buddy and I jacked up the
rear end of the coupe a mean-looking 2 inches. All right, so the girls were
not exactly lining up at the root beer stand to beg for rides in my hot
machine. But there was one evening when I knew the dough I had dropped
spiffing up the Merc had been well spent: That was when one of the car-hops
stopped to check her hair and makeup in the mirror-like finish of one of my
baby moon hubcaps.

The same thing is true of deer decoys. Any decoy on the market will
attract deer, but with a little doctoring, your decoy will be even more attrac-
tive. You can do three things to increase a decoy's effectiveness: Add scent,
provide movement and enhance realism. Let's take a look at each of these.

Making Decoys Smell Like Deer

The first step in scenting a decoy so it smells like the real thing is to make
sure it does not smell like you. All of the deer scent in the world will not
cover up human odor, so it's imperative that the decoy be odor-free from the
start.

To accomplish this, I store my decoys where they won't absorb foreign
odors during the off-season. Then, a week before I plan to use them, I place
my decoys in the backyard and let Mother Nature do her thing with rain, sun
and lots of fresh air. When I handle my decoys in the field, I usually wear
rubber gloves. If I forget my rubber gloves, I handle the decoy with a pair of
clean cloth gloves.

After setting up the decoy, I spray it down with an odor-eliminator. If you
think all of this is going a little overboard, you've probably never had a big
buck come to your decoy, catch a whiff of human odor, and bolt as if stuck
with a cattle prod. I've had that happen, and I don't ever want it to happen

Although deer are attracted visually to the decoy, the author recommends always applying a scent near the decoy and scent-killer on the decoy. These steps will increase the amount of time a deer will hang around the decoy.

again.

It's not necessary to place scent on the ground near your decoy. Deer are attracted visually to the decoy. That fact doesn't change, scent or no scent. However, I always use scent because they usually increase the amount of time a deer will hang around the decoy. The longer I can get a buck to hang around the decoy, the better the odds he will present a shooting opportunity. That's especially important when bow-hunting, because the added attraction of scent keeps the buck preoccupied and allows me to draw my bow.

When I started using decoys, I applied scent directly to them. This worked fine, but as I discovered, placing scent directly on a decoy has some major drawbacks. I often stash my decoy in the woods between hunts when I know I'm going to hunt the same stand or another stand nearby in the next day or so. I usually hide the decoy in a deadfall or in the bottom of a gully. Tracks in the mud and snow have shown me that deer find my decoy no matter where I hide it if the decoy has deer scent on it. I can't prove it, but I think it's possible that deer finding my hidden decoy become leery and won't approach it when I place it near my stand while hunting.

Another drawback is that it's difficult to remove deer scent from a decoy.

Some hunters rub a piece of apple on the nose of the decoy to make it more alluring to whitetails when they approach.

As a result, I've had experiences where the scent rubbed off on my clothing when I carried the decoy to and from the woods. I'm a fanatic when it comes to keeping my clothing scent-free, and the last thing I want on my clothing is buck or doe scent.

Some hunters sprinkle scent on the ground around their decoys, but I believe I get better results if I keep the scent above the ground. I like to take a 1- or 2-foot stick and push it into the ground near the decoy's rump. If I'm using a buck decoy, I hang a tarsal gland on the stick. A tarsal gland holds its natural musky odor a long time and there's no need to add additional scent. If I don't have a tarsal gland, I use commercial tarsal-gland scent.

For doe decoys, I use estrous doe urine. When I'm done hunting, I put the tarsal gland or scent wick into an airtight plastic bag until the next hunt. It's wise to store tarsal glands in a refrigerator or on ice between hunts.

Another neat trick is to rub an apple slice or the meat of an acorn on the

Movement adds realism to any decoy, and the author experiences far fewer hang-ups when he attaches something to the decoy that will move. A piece of white tape or a handkerchief tacked to the deer will help mimic tail movements.

decoy's nose. Deer often touch noses when greeting each other, and it's common for a deer to sniff a decoy's nose. I've never had the acorn or apple scent spook a deer. In fact, I've watched deer lick the nose of my decoy. On one occasion, a fawn tried to bite the nose off a decoy that I had doctored with an apple slice!

Adding Movement

Movement adds realism to any decoy. Many times I've watched a buck approach a decoy and then hang up out of bow range while staring at it. I believe bucks hang up because they're waiting for the other deer to make the next move. I experience far fewer hang-ups when I add some motion to my decoy. Today, I rarely hunt over a decoy that isn't rigged for some type of motion.

When I first started messing around with decoys, I attached toilet paper to the ears and tail of my decoy to provide movement. Toilet paper works great, fluttering in the slightest breeze, until it gets damp. Rain isn't the only thing that makes toilet paper worthless. Fog, a fine mist or light snow is all it takes to ruin this tactic.

Then I experimented with white feathers. They work better than paper, but if it's raining, forget it. Wet feathers don't cut it.

I found the solution to the weather problems after much trial and error — a white plastic garbage bag. Buy the cheapest you can find, because the

Many times I've watched a buck approach a decoy and then hang up out of bow range to stare at it. I can't prove it, but I think it's waiting for the other deer to make the next move.

cheap ones use the thinnest plastic, which is why they rip open and leave your garbage strewn all over the kitchen when you lift them out of the waste basket! But that same irritating quality makes them flutter in a gentle breeze. Cut pieces that are a half-inch wide by 4 inches long. I attach one strip to each ear and another to the tail or rump.

Duct tape works well for attaching the strips to the decoy, but I prefer to use small finishing nails. On a hard-plastic decoy, I use a cigarette lighter to melt a soft spot or small hole in the decoy and then push the nail into the desired spot.

Plastic strips are cheap and easy to make, and as long as you have some wind, they're effective at adding movement in all weather.

The ultimate in motion and realism, however, might be the robotic decoys made by Custom Robotic Wildlife. This company began its operation by making robotic decoys for conservation wardens working road-hunting setups. Serious deer hunters soon discovered the robots worked just as well in fooling deer. These amazing imitations feature a tanned deer hide and detachable antlers.

Check your state's regulations before using them, however. Electronic decoys and decoying devices aren't legal everywhere. Where they are legal, though, they're effective — and a barrel of fun. The top-end model features a head that turns and a tail that flicks by remote control. If you get one of these, I suggest using the head turn to convince deer they're looking at the real thing. Just toggle the remote control switch lightly. You don't want the head to turn fast; just a slow move works best.

The decoy's tail, I learned, should only be flicked when the deer is at a distance and there is some "covering" wind. That's because the tail makes a slight sound when activated, which will turn deer inside out if they're close enough to hear it.

The Tail Wagger is a battery-operated device that attaches easily to most decoys, especially the Carry-Lite and Flambeau models. The Tail Wagger allows the hunter to set a timer so that the tail wags from side to side at a pre-set interval. Eight seconds is one example. When a buck hangs up and stares at the decoy, he soon sees the tail twitch from side to side, just like real deer

When the author sets up silhouette decoys, he uses duct tape to secure a strip of white plastic to the ear and rump.

do all of the time. Bingo, the deer has seen what it wanted to see.

Some hunters even replace the Tail Wagger's foam tail with a real deer tail for even more realism.

The Tail Wagger's tail is painted to resemble a real deer's tail — brown laced with white. Using a tip from New York outdoor writer Charles Alsheimer, I learned the tail works better when it's turned around so the all-white side is showing. Deer spot the movement better with the white side showing. In states where it's legal, the Tail Wagger is a slick way of adding realistic motion to your decoy.

The Higdon Motion Deer Decoy has a cord that extends from the decoy, which is a silhouette, to your tree stand. When a deer is reluctant to come to the motionless decoy, you can pull the cord to move the decoy's head up and down. This decoy works well, but I've found the cord can get hung up on brush and limbs when hunting from a tree stand. One thing you can do that helps is to run the cord to the bottom of your tree and run it through an eye bolt and then straight up to your stand. If you hunt from a ground blind, working the Higdon decoy is really easy.

On silhouette decoys like those from Mel Dutton, Outlaw and Higdon, a stiff breeze can cause the decoy to shimmy and shutter on its stake, which is all you need to convince a reluctant buck that he's looking at the real thing. When I use silhouettes, I use duct tape to secure a strip of white plastic to the ear and the rump.

Ten years ago, if you would have asked me what the most important aspect of any decoy is, I would have said authenticity. If you ask me that same question today, my reply would be movement.

Another trick is to tie a string to a bush or sapling near the decoy and jerk the string to make the bush move.

However, the ultimate in movement is the robotic decoy. Robotic deer are made from the real thing — a life-size mount that's been rigged with electronics. Robotic deer, used extensively by conservation officers to nab poachers, feature remote controls that hunters can operate easily from tree stands and ground blinds.

Although I know some hunters who never use any movement on their decoys, I believe decoy movement can do nothing but improve your chances of duping cautious bucks.

The Importance of Realism

Ten years ago, if you would have asked me what was the most important aspect of any decoy, I would have said authenticity. The more a decoy looks like the real thing, the more likely real deer are going to accept it as real. However, ask me that same question today, and I would say movement is nearly as important. Although I still believe realistic decoys attract more deer, I now believe that authenticity runs a close second to movement when it comes to tripping a buck's trigger.

Does that mean anything that remotely resembles a deer will work? Sometimes, but not consistently. Realistic decoys attract more deer and hold their attention longer than do decoys that are less realistic in appearance.

One of the first decoys I ever hunted over was a McKenzie target over which a deer hide had been stretched and tacked down. We added glass eyes, like those used by taxidermists in mounts. Completing the ruse was an 8-point rack that measured about 130 inches. We named the decoy Rufus. Several times when I dozed off on stand and awoke to see him standing in front of me, my heart sprang to my throat and my hand reached for my bow.

Rufus looked so real that he even fooled me! Unfortunately, he was about as portable as an anvil.

CHAPTER 15

Reading Deer Body Language When Using Decoys

The ability to read a deer's body language is important to any deer hunter, but I believe it's even more important when hunting over a decoy. If you have the ability to know what the various body postures mean in the whitetail's world, you can react accordingly.

Many old-timers know what a deer is going to do before the deer actually does it. How? They've learned to read body language and anticipate the deer's next move. This chapter explains common postures deer use when approaching decoys and how you should react to each situation.

The "I'm Big and I'm Bad" Posture

A buck will often approach a decoy with his ears pinned back, the hair standing up on his neck and back, and walking sideways like the Duke used to do when he sauntered into a saloon full of bad guys. The buck is trying to persuade the fake deer to vamoose.

I've seen a few bucks so worked up that drool hung from their mouths as they strutted onto the scene. When you see a buck looking this ornery, there's about a 50 percent chance it will attack your decoy. Your best move is to take the first good shot the buck offers. Bucks sometimes hang around after attacking decoys, but not usually.

The Stare

In the world of golf, Raymond Floyd and Greg Norman have it — the stare. In the wild, the white-tailed deer is the master of the stare. Oftentimes a buck will approach a decoy and then stop and stand stone still for a minute, sometimes longer. The buck will typically

Curious bucks are typically on high alert when they approach decoys. Therefore, be prepared to shoot when given a chance. Bucks that walk away from decoys seldom return.

focus on the situation before him while cupping his ears forward in an attempt to intercept the softest grunt from the fake buck. The stare unnerves a lot of hunters and causes them to make mistakes. Just remember, you can win the contest if you don't move.

Two things here: First, don't move. Not even an eyelash. Second, don't stare back at the buck. I'm convinced a deer can sense that eye-to-eye predatory contact. Humans sometimes get a similar feeling that someone is watching us. If you don't move and you avoid the temptation to stare at the buck, odds are good you'll be treated to this next bit of whitetail body language.

The Tail Flick

After standing still for any period of time, a deer will nearly always flick its tail before taking the next step. If you're just getting ready to shoot at a standing deer and it flicks its tail, you have about

A buck will often approach a decoy with his ears pinned back and the hair standing up on his neck and back. A buck uses this aggressive posture in an attempt to intimidate competitors.

one second to make a decision: Either shoot immediately or wait until the buck stops again.

He Ain't Coming Back

Here is a situation that sure had me confused. In fact, it cost me a shot at a big buck. I had a 10-pointer side-walking around my decoy in that "I'm-big-and-bad" mode. I knew all I had to do was calm myself long enough to make the shot when the buck stopped. I had hiked a long way to get to my stand, and, out of convenience, I had carried a silhouette decoy instead of a full-body decoy.

When the buck got face to face with the decoy, the deer in front of him all of a sudden disappeared — or at least became the skinniest deer he had ever seen! This disappearing act does not usually faze bucks, but this buck reacted negatively. He turned, and with his hair still bristled and his ears laid back, he walked off in that distinct

Scent control is crucial when hunting over decoys. That's why it's wise to handle your decoy with rubber gloves and to douse it with scent-eliminating spray before heading to your tree stand.

A doe that comes to a decoy and doesn't like what she sees will do what I call the "high step" as she leaves. In this case, the doe lifts each front hoof up high, cocking it like a rifle hammer, and then slams it to the ground.

stiff-legged gait. He never looked back.

I made two mistakes on that buck. First, he had offered a good shot when he came around the front of my decoy. However, I passed in hopes of getting a perfect opportunity. Second, when he walked off with that "I'm bad" posture, I expected him to turn and come right back. I've learned since that once a buck detects something fishy with a decoy setup, he ain't coming back.

Does are another story. I've never seen a doe engage in the same stiff-legged, ears-laid-back, hairs-erect posturing that bucks use. A doe that comes to a decoy and doesn't like what she sees will do what I call the "high step" as she leaves. In this case, the doe lifts each front hoof up high, cocking it like a rifle hammer, and then slams it to the ground. This is how an old biddy warns other deer that something isn't quite right.

These does will also usually throw in some serious snorting. As is so common with does, they just can't seem to put it behind them, either. I've often watched suspicious does slowly circling my stand while snorting, stamping their hoofs and basically ruining everything I had going. On two occasions I actually climbed down from my stand and scared them away. Of course, there's a more permanent solution to the problem if you have a doe tag in your pocket!

CHAPTER 16

Deadly Setups for Decoys

Farm country is ideally suited to decoying deer. Typical farm country is a mosaic of crop fields, scattered woodlots and creek and river bottoms. Of course the amount of wooded cover — as opposed to standing crops — varies greatly by region. But everywhere I've hunted farmland deer, there have always been plenty of edges and openings for positioning decoys.

White-tailed deer are creatures of the edge. They travel along edges and feed on the new growth that is most prevalent at the fringe of fields, draws and woodlots. Isn't it nice that those edges also make ideal locations for setting up a decoy?

Farm country is full of places ideally suited to decoying deer. In addition to an abundance of edge cover, farms have fence lines, waterways, skinny creek bottoms, drainage ditches, windbreaks and tree lines, all of which are used by deer to move from one place to another. It's usually not too difficult to find a place where deer can spot your decoy from a distance.

Decoys in the Suburbs
Another habitat type ideally suited for decoys is North America's ever-expanding suburbs. It's no secret that the ever-adaptable whitetail gets along all too well in our suburbs. When those cute little deer begin mowing down expensive shrubbery and going "thwhuuuummmp" on the bumpers of SUVs and BMWs, the cry goes out to wildlife agencies to do something about those pesky deer. Wildlife managers often turn to archers to help control the deer population. This creates a wonderful opportunity for us to show nonhunters that we're thoughtful and ethical.

Whenever I get a chance to hunt suburban deer, I always go out of my way to maintain a low profile. I park my vehicle where it will not be noticed by every homeowner going to or coming home from work, even if it means parking a good hike from where I plan to hunt. I slip into and out of the woods as unobtrusively as possible.

No, I'm not trying to hide the fact I'm a hunter. I'm proud of that fact, but I've learned the hard way that I have other people to consider

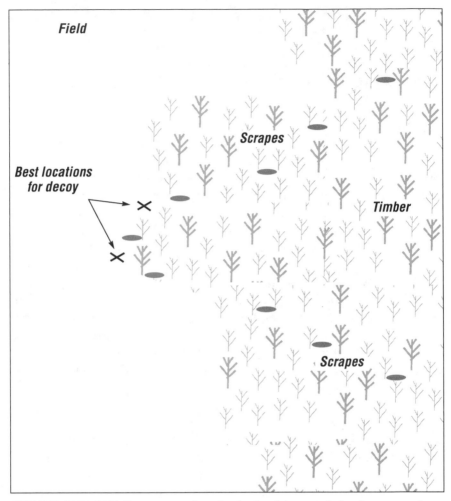

SCRAPE LINE SET: *Because mature bucks tend to scent-check scrapes from downwind instead of walking right into the scrape, a decoy placed along the scrape line can help coax a cautious buck within shooting range. Remember, a decoy must be visible to be effective. For that reason, it's best to place the decoy along the field edge, as shown.*

than just the landowner or two who gave me permission to hunt. Even though I'm not straying from those properties, my presence in the neighborhood is not appreciated by everyone. I've lost a couple of good spots because of the pressure that neighbors put on the owners who gave me permission. So I've become careful not to draw any unwanted attention.

Another thing I do when hunting in suburbs is to take only high-

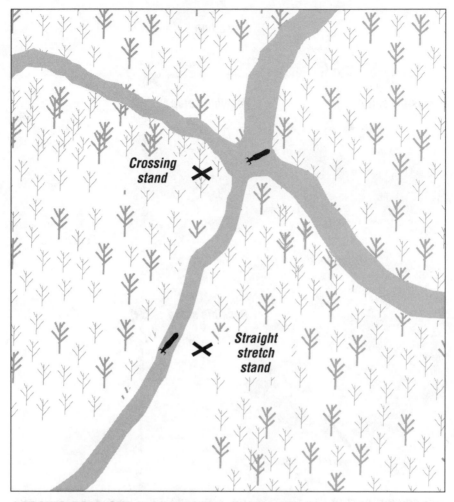

LOGGING ROAD SET: In big woods or forest settings, a logging road might provide your only opening for a decoy. To ensure maximum visibility of the decoy, place it along long, straight stretches of the logging road or — even better — where two logging roads intersect.

percentage shots that will kill quickly. Naturally, this is something I strive for in any hunting situation, but when hunting suburbs, I'm extra careful. I refuse to take any shot past 20 yards, even though I practice a lot and am proficient at twice that distance.

A properly positioned decoy helps draw deer in close, and gives you that perfect angle for shots that result in clean, quick kills.

When hunting in the suburbs, I usually use a doe decoy. The reason is that for most of my suburban hunts, I'm trying to kill mature does.

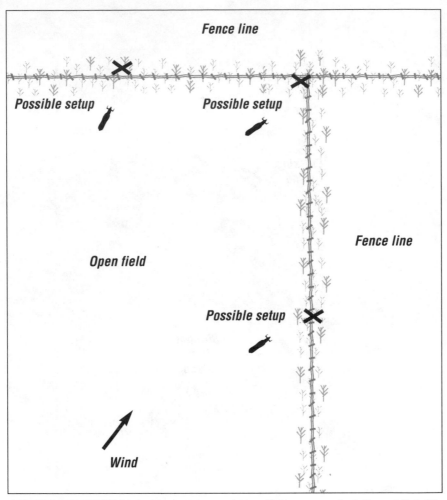

***FENCE-LINE SETUPS:** In farm country, fence lines are part of the whitetail's network of highways. A decoy set along a well-traveled fence line will get some attention. But for maximum results, set up where the decoy is visible from intersecting fence lines.*

If controlling the herd is the goal — and it is in most suburbs — then shooting mature does is the best management tool. Does are attracted to doe decoys, but will frequently avoid a buck decoy.

At the same time, a doe decoy does not hurt my chances of decoying in a good buck. Bucks will come into a doe decoy just fine. As we discussed earlier, doe decoys tend to attract too many deer, which isn't what you want on hunts where you're targeting mature bucks instead of mature does.

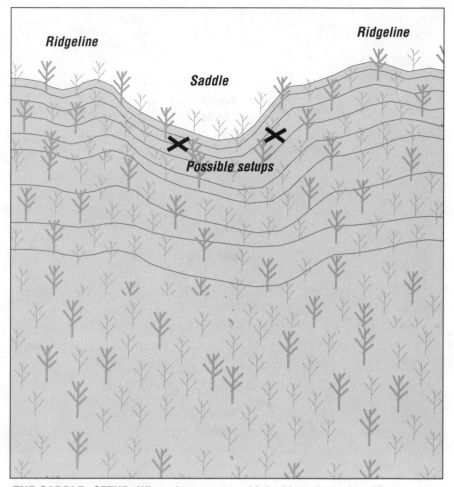

THE SADDLE SETUP: *When deer cross a high ridge, they often like to shoot the gap through a "saddle" or low spot on the ridgeline. Such saddles make perfect spots to set up a decoy.*

In most suburban hunting situations, you don't need a decoy to attract deer from a distance. That's because deer are confined to small parcels and strips of cover. They'll often have no choice but to pass fairly close to your stand. On most of my suburban hunts, the decoy's main function is to help position a deer at the perfect shooting angle and hold its attention while I draw and make a smooth release.

Decoying in the Big Woods
The opposite extremes in deer habitat are forests and big woods. When

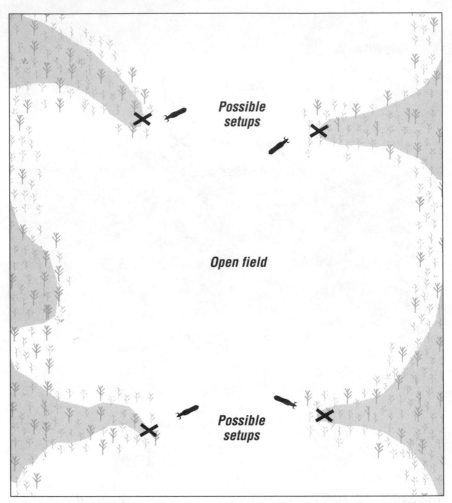

CONNECTING POINTS: *In many areas, erosion has formed gullies or ditches that jut out into fields on ridgetops or in valleys. Over the years, gullies often grow in with brush and trees. Deer that cross fields often start their crossing from one tip of a gully and head straight across to another gully. These connecting points are ideal sites for decoy setups.*

I'm hunting big woods, I rely heavily on calling, rattling and decoys. In most cases, deer densities in the big woods is on the low side. This usually makes for far more difficult hunting conditions than the suburbs and farmlands. When you're hunting a blend of agricultural land, river bottoms and woodlots — places where it's not uncommon for deer densities to run 20 to 40 deer or more per square mile, you'll probably see some deer even if you never use a call, decoy or rattling horns. The

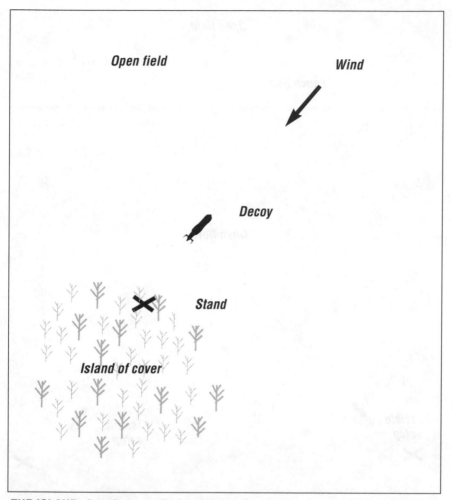

THE ISLAND: *Any time you find an island of cover surrounded by an open area, you're looking at a potentially excellent decoy setup. Especially during the rut, bucks will cross open areas as they search for does. Island setups are also good early and late in the season when deer are feeding in fields and clear-cuts. A lone tree or a small clump of trees in a field or clear-cut will also work, as will a rock pile, an old windmill, or even abandoned farm machinery. Another possibility is to create your own island with a blind or hay bales.*

fact is, you'll see more deer in "civilized" regions just because of the sheer numbers of deer.

But in the big woods, deer densities are usually much lower. In the forested regions of Saskatchewan, for instance, deer densities are nearly always in single digits, sometimes less than five deer per square mile.

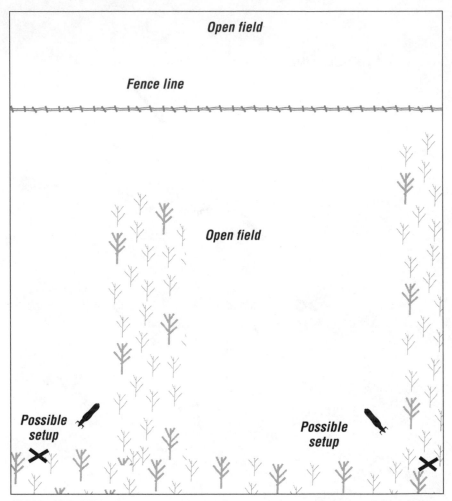

FIELD CORNERS: *Almost anywhere along a field can be a good place for a decoy setup, but the author prefers corners. Bucks often cut field corners, which makes them great spots for decoys. In addition, a corner provides two edges for increased visibility of the decoy.*

When you're faced with a lot of country and not many deer, calling, rattling and decoying are not just tools you use to spice up the action. They might well mean the difference between seeing a deer and counting trees out of sheer boredom.

Another thing I've noticed about decoying deer in the big woods is that forest deer almost never pass up a chance to visit a decoy. It would be a stretch to call them lonesome, but I think it's fair to say that because deer in low-density herds have less frequent contact with other deer than

Big-woods deer are more inclined to saunter over for a visit when they spot what they think is another real deer.

do their counterparts in higher-density regions, big-woods deer are more inclined to saunter over for a visit when they spot what they think is another deer.

I'm also convinced big-woods bucks are more easily lured with deer calls, rattling antlers and decoys during the rut than are their farmland cousins. I think it's a matter of opportunity. A breeder buck living in the big timber has to do some serious cruising to encounter a hot doe. When he hears, smells or sees anything that might indicate an estrous doe, you have his undivided attention.

Decoying works on big-woods whitetails, but not every stand is suited to using a decoy. In order for a decoy to be most effective, it needs to be placed so deer can see it from a distance, and the farther the better. Big timber, by its nature, does not lend itself to long-distance viewing. But if you keep your eyes open for places where decoying will work, you'll be amazed at the number of places where a decoy will enhance the hunting.

CHAPTER 17

Favorite Hunts of the Decoy Masters

As with any other aspect of deer hunting, a favorite part of decoying is sharing the excitement with other hunters in the form of deer stories. You show me a hunter who lives for deer season, and chances are I'll show you a hunter who loves to tell and hear deer stories. Story-telling is as rooted in deer hunting as gun powder and arrow heads.

Let's begin our chapter of deer hunting stories with Kevin Smith:

Kevin Smith

Kevin Smith is a friend of mine who lives in Indiana. He's a good hunter and has been hunting over a decoy for about 10 years.

Unlike most deer hunters who use decoys, Smith uses a doe decoy instead of a buck decoy. When bow-hunting, he sets the decoy within 10 yards of his stand. When hunting with a firearm, he places it up to 70 yards away. He rarely rattles or calls, and he uses no scents.

What follows are Smith's stories behind three bucks he killed while using a decoy.

Smith Remembers "The Golden-Haired Buck"

In Fall 1991, our bow season in northeastern Indiana was well into fall before the weather finally cooled off and the first rut signs appeared. I'm fortunate enough to have good hunting land with some trophy bucks within a mile of my home. Snow was falling on the gray underbrush as I strained to see in the first blush of day in late October. I spotted a small buck about 100 yards out in a nearby CRP field. Then a doe stepped from the bedding cover north of my stand.

The small buck looked at the doe and then abruptly snapped his head around to stare into some heavy cover. When the small buck took off like a scared cat, I knew a bigger buck was probably around. Within seconds a beautiful 8-pointer emerged and strolled to the center of the field. The buck had a golden coat and bleached antlers, which would probably go 140 inches on the Boone and Crockett Club's scale.

Kevin Smith of Indiana prefers using doe decoys. When bow-hunting, he places the decoy within 10 yards of his stand. For gun-hunting, he places it up to 70 yards away. He rarely rattles or calls, and he never uses scents.

My eyes were riveted on the buck, but I caught a slight movement to the side. I nearly fell out of my tree when I turned to see the biggest buck I had ever seen! He had a 10-point rack with excellent mass, and I was sure he would score in the 160s. The big buck and the 8-pointer postured for each other before the 8-pointer got the message and ran off. For the next hour, the big buck put on a show as he cleared the area of all other deer except the doe, which must have been in estrus.

When I grunted at him, he and the doe moved around my position until the monster buck stood 18 yards away. Unfortunately, there was no way to get an arrow through the dense multiflora rose. All I could do was wait and hope the buck would move into the open. But after about 20 minutes, the buck and the doe disappeared into the heavy cover. I never saw him again, but I felt blessed just to have seen the show he put on.

A month later, my in-laws asked what I wanted for Christmas. I usually just circle something in the Cabela's catalog, and that year I circled a Flambeau deer decoy. They thoughtfully ordered it early enough so I could use it before Christmas. A few days after receiving the decoy, I gave it a try during the shotgun season. The land I hunt is

My first experience with decoying whitetails took place about 1985 when I built a crude doe decoy out of cardboard and masking tape. I used it for an ill-fated attempt to sneak up on deer feeding in an alfalfa field.
— Lee Lakosky

private property, and because no other hunters would be on the property, I felt safe using the decoy.

I knew nothing about using deer decoys, so I just put it out on a small sand hill that overlooked a clearing in the woods I was hunting. Then everything started going wrong. When I climbed into my permanent stand and sat down, the 5-gallon bucket I use for a seat cracked loudly. I was sure the loud noise from that frozen bucket would spook any nearby deer. Minutes later, I was startled to hear the roar of a diesel engine as a large tractor started plowing a field about 200 yards away. The evening was not going as planned!

I didn't have much time to dwell on my bad luck. A doe slipped through the woods 60 yards away. Then I glimpsed another deer coming my way. It was a buck and, judging by the short look I had at one side of its rack, it was good one. When the buck stepped onto a trail I had brush-hogged, he stopped and stared at the decoy. I settled the cross-hairs behind the buck's near shoulder and missed him cleanly, but he was so focused on the decoy that he never moved. My second shot dropped the buck in his tracks.

I left the stand like a firefighter sliding down the pole, and was standing over the dead buck in seconds. He was the biggest buck I had ever killed. I recognized him as the golden-coated 8-pointer from that magical morning in October. The buck weighed 197 pounds field dressed, and his rack had a gross score of 139⅞.

Another 8-Pointer

In 1993, nearly two years after taking that big 8-pointer, I was on a stand in that same woods on an evening in late October. My decoy was eight steps in front of my stand.

Because the cover was thick around my stand, I had brush-hogged a few trails around the stand for shooting lanes. I had positioned the decoy on one of those trails.

I suddenly heard a twig snap behind me, and turned in time to see an

His eyes locked onto the decoy, and he stepped back into the woods. When his head passed behind a tree, I drew my bow and waited. At 23 yards he stopped to stare at the decoy again, and I released my arrow.
— Kevin Smith

8-pointer jump a fence and land on the trail about 25 yards behind me. His eyes locked onto the decoy, and then he stepped off the trail and back into the woods. When his head passed behind a big tree, I drew my bow and waited. At 23 yards the buck stopped to stare at the decoy again, and I released my arrow. The broadhead did its job. The buck went only 30 yards before crashing. My decoy was my new best friend.

The Biggest of All
On Oct. 22, 1995, my dad, Henry, and I, along with a few friends, were flying in a private plane headed for Schefferville, Quebec, to hunt caribou. Our plane crashed, but miraculously, none of us was killed. Ten hours after the crash, a helicopter rescued us.

Because of fractured vertebrae in my neck, it was Nov. 11 before I was able to shoot my bow. The rut was in full swing and I was anxious to be hunting again. I chose a permanent stand overlooking a 30-acre CRP field with a small creek running through its center.

It was a chore carrying my decoy because of my sore neck, but I managed and set the decoy in front of my stand before climbing in. The first deer I saw was a doe feeding about 100 yards out in the field. About 45 minutes later, the doe had fed to within 60 yards of my stand when I noticed movement behind her. A huge buck materialized.

I had to get my arrow around the other side of the tree trunk to prepare for the shot. Inch by cautious inch, I made my move. By the time I was in position, the doe was only 20 yards away and the buck was right behind her.

The doe spotted my doe decoy and dismissed it as no threat. When the buck saw the decoy, he stared at it for a long time and then turned to follow his doe. I forced myself not to stare at his antlers, and then drew and released.

I waited four hours, assembled some friends and then went looking for him. He was lying 15 yards from where I last glimpsed him. The buck, which field dressed 229 pounds had a net score of 164 Pope and Young, and was the second-highest scoring deer killed in Indiana that year.

Dennis Williams

Dennis Williams is a Minnesota deer hunter who makes a habit of shooting impressive bucks in his home state and other places. This hunt was Williams' first experience with a decoy. I'm sure it won't be his last.

Duping a Buck in Velvet

On an early-season hunt in western Manitoba, my guide had seen a buck use the same trail on two occasions. With a favorable wind the next evening, I placed the buck decoy downwind of the trail and down-wind of my ground

Dennis Williams of Minnesota defied the odds by duping an early-season buck while bow-hunting in Manitoba. Some hunters don't like using decoys early in the season because the fake deer tend to spook bucks not yet stoked with testosterone.

blind. I was hoping the buck would exit on the trail and then be forced to walk in front of me to get to the decoy. About 1½ hours before sunset, a couple of does and fawns fed into the field and milled around the decoy for a while before winding me, possibly because of all the bug spray I had put on to keep the mosquitoes at bay.

At sunset I caught some movement where the trail entered the field, but the deer just stood at the edge of the field, partially concealed in the brush for two minutes. When the buck finally moved, it swung its head

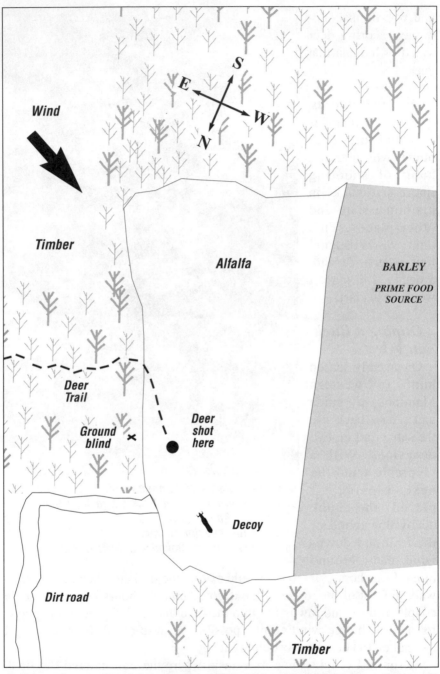

A thorough scouting job by Dennis Williams' guide helped them figure out where the buck was likely to appear. They positioned the decoy past the ambush site to lure the buck past Williams' ground blind.

Lee Lakosky of Minnesota used homemade decoys when he first tried decoying deer in the mid-1980s. After he began to use commercial decoys, he saw his success increase after adding a Tail Wagger unit to fool deer that would otherwise be wary of the decoy.

around and I got a look at its impressive rack. The buck spotted my decoy, and without hesitation walked toward it.

I drew my bow when the buck's head was behind a tree. I was about to grunt to try to stop him in my shooting lane when he stopped on his own. With the buck broadside at 30 yards and concentrating on the decoy, I took my time lining up the shot and made a smooth release. When the arrow sliced through him, the buck whirled and ran back on the trail he had just left. I heard him crash a short distance into the woods.

The beautiful 5-by-5 was in full velvet and had a gross score of 160⅝. That was only my first experience with a decoy, but you can bet it won't be my last!

Lee Lakosky

Lee Lakosky is another Minnesota boy with a passion for bow-hunting mature whitetails. Decoying is one of the tactics he uses with success. Here, he describes what works and what doesn't:

With a few minutes of shooting light left, the buck spotted my doe decoy and came on the trot. Everything looked perfect until I realized I had put the decoy too close to the base of the tree where I was perched.
— Mark Kayser

Motion Makes a Difference

My first experience with decoying whitetails took place about 1985 when I built a crude doe decoy out of cardboard and masking tape. I used this decoy in what proved to be an ill-fated attempt to sneak up on deer feeding in an alfalfa field near my home.

While my first attempt at decoying was far from a success, I was convinced the idea had merit. Some years later I bought a Flambeau Redi-Doe, and my success at decoying deer within range increased. However, I still had some deer, especially mature animals, that would stare and stare at the motionless decoy. When they were finally convinced the unmoving animal wasn't for real, they would detour around the decoy. Because I was concentrating on big bucks, I didn't want to risk any of my hunts, so I retired the decoy to the garage rafters.

Last year I bought a Tail Wagger unit and installed it on my decoy. The motion of the tail seemed to take care of the suspicious animals. I had numerous deer walk up to or past my decoy. I also had several young to middle-aged bucks knock the tail off of my decoy with their noses. I had to laugh as one young 10-pointer tried to mount my decoy. If the way the deer reacted to the decoy with the Tail Wagger is any indication, I expect great things from this device in the future.

Mark Kayser

Mark Kayser, who lives in Pierre, S.D., is a veteran deer hunter who has been using decoys for many years.

Jumping on a Pattern

As the rut approaches, it's time to get serious about using a decoy. But you can't just set out a decoy any old place and hope to have a big deer come over to investigate. Proper decoying methods need to be employed to eliminate mistakes before they happen.

I'll never forget the shot I ruined at a real brute of a buck because of

Mark Kayser of South Dakota has spent many years using deer decoys. He thinks a good time to use decoys is when the rut winds down. An alert decoy will still attract some bucks looking for does, and a grazing decoy works well when winter arrives and deer start feeding earlier in the day.

my inexperience with decoys. On a drizzly November morning, I left an area after seeing no deer, and climbed into a tree stand in a thick patch of timber to try some rattling. No sooner had I brought my antlers together than a huge buck with distinctive kickers on each G2 rose from his bed just 40 yards away. All I could do was stay still and watch. Within a few minutes the buck slipped away.

I knew the buck didn't know I had been the source of the sound, so for the next three evenings I spied on the buck from a long distance using my spotting scope. Each evening, the buck traveled the same edge of a field, making scrapes and searching for a hot doe. Confident I had him pegged, I hung my stand in a cottonwood along that field edge and put my decoy under the tree. The buck appeared right on schedule and went along the field edge freshening scrapes.

With a few minutes of shooting light left, the buck finally spotted my doe decoy and came on the trot. Everything looked perfect until I realized I had put the decoy too close to the base of the cottonwood where I was perched. With the buck directly underneath me, I sent my arrow zipping over his back. I never saw that buck again, except in my dreams.

But I learned from that mistake. By 1994, I was focusing all of my rut-hunting time on hunting over a decoy. On the evening of Nov. 10 that

One drawback of hunting with decoys is that they must be carried to the hunting site. The inconvenience of lugging a decoy around, however, will quickly be forgotten the first time a buck comes in to check things out.

year, I positioned my Flambeau Redi-Doe, which I had equipped with antlers, in a thicket that always produced rutting activity. I was barely settled into my stand when I spotted a nice buck about 100 yards away. I hit him with a series of grunts and he hurried in my direction.

At just 30 yards, a brush pile hid my decoy from the buck's sight. He seemed to lose interest, so I gave him a couple more grunts. That did it! The buck plowed straight through the pile of brush and came at the

At just 30 yards, a brush pile hid my decoy from the buck. He seemed to lose interest, so I gave him a couple more grunts. That did it! The buck plowed straight through the pile of brush and came at the decoy.
— Mark Kayser

decoy with his ears laid back and hackles standing straight. Before he could launch his attack, I sent an arrow zipping through his chest. The buck ran 40 yards, turned to take a last look at the decoy and toppled.

Don't forget about using a decoy even as the rut winds down. An alert decoy will still attract some bucks looking for does, and a grazing decoy works well when winter arrives and deer are forced to feed earlier in the day. During the 1993 season, winter arrived early and deer were feeding early in the evening.

After setting up my tree stand along the deer's travel route, I put my decoy along the trail. On the fifth night I hunted the stand, a large 8-point buck trotted over to see what the decoy had found to munch on, and offered me a perfect shot.

Kayser's Tips

✓ Decoys work, but they won't take the place of scouting or solid hunting techniques.

✓ Have patience. Nothing works all of the time, and decoying is no exception.

✓ When using a doe decoy, face the decoy away from you. When using a buck decoy, face the decoy toward your stand. About 15 to 20 yards is my favorite distance when bow-hunting.

Ian McMurchy

Ian McMurchy lives in Regina, Saskatchewan, the heart of monster buck country. Besides being an exceptional wildlife photographer and accomplished writer, McMurchy has a lot of experience hunting and photographing over decoys.

Which One is Real?

When you buy a deer decoy, proper hunting etiquette requires you give your new hunting buddy a name. When Flambeau came on the market with its Redi-Doe decoy many years ago, I did much of the initial field-

This photo was taken in 1992 by Ian McMurchy. McMurchy was one of the first hunters to widely use decoys. He talked this Pennsylvania hunter into trying his decoy "Darlene" during a hunt in the forests of Saskatchewan. This buck postured and displayed for the decoy before approaching too close to the waiting muzzle-loading hunter.

testing and photographing of the product.

I nicknamed my decoy "Old Darlene." This decoy fooled many bucks and does, and did a great job for many years. Celebrities hunted with her, bucks tried to cozy up to her (and more), does licked her nose and many deer accepted her as a newcomer to the herd. When Old Darlene tried on a set of antlers, she was attacked and knocked over. She caused some marvelous territorial displays. Unfortunately, she wore out with time. Her joints got brittle, her color faded and she started to wobble in the wind. I replaced her with a couple of new decoys. But, like my little wife, there will only be one Darlene.

Old Darlene sometimes gave me fits. I remember one hunt, in particular. I had spotted a nice buck and a doe partially hidden in a low dip in a harvested wheat field. I saw them as I still-hunted along an old trail that ran to the field through heavy cover. I slipped into the aspens to avoid detection and tried to silently close the distance. After a 20-minute sneak, I slowly worked my way to the edge of the bluff and looked for a sturdy tree to serve as a shooting rest for my muzzleloader.

After one last look to check on the deer, I would get in position to take the shot. I slowly brought the binoculars to my eyes and focused on the deer. Then I started to laugh. I had just put the sneak on my own decoys!

The previous evening, my hunting partner had hunted over the decoys

After one last look to check on the deer, I would get in position to take the shot. I brought the binoculars to my eyes and focused on the deer. Then I started to laugh. I had just put the sneak on my own decoys!
— Ian McMurchy

and left them out overnight with the intention of hunting over them again in the morning. Unfortunately, the next morning, my partner was sick, so I had gone hunting on my own.

David Westmoreland

David Westmoreland of Missouri, like many good hunters, was slow to come around to decoying. But once he got started, there was no stopping him.

The Excitement Never Ends

After years of reading about decoying deer and seeing some amazing footage shot by other hunters, I eventually decided it was time to try it. I had been using decoys for turkeys for years, and had never paid much attention to decoy placement. I assumed the same approach would work for deer. I bought the Delta 2D tail-wagging decoy, stuck it out in front of my stand, and waited for big bucks to come running. After several days of hunting and a couple of different bucks passing by, I couldn't understand why they weren't coming to my decoy.

My stand was on the edge of a thick bedding area, and there was a lot of heavy brush around my stand. While sitting around one night wondering what I was going to do the next morning, it dawned on me. If a buck couldn't see the decoy, he would probably not come in. That got me thinking about a fencerow I had hunted earlier. I had seen a couple of big bucks cross the field I was sitting on, but they had not come close enough to the fencerow for a shot. The next morning I was set up in that fencerow with my decoy about 30 yards away on the edge of the freshly cut cornfield.

I wanted the decoy far enough away from the fencerow to be visible to any buck crossing the field. Shortly after first light, two yearling does began working down the field edge. When they spotted the decoy, they started bobbing their heads and working closer in a circling fashion.

When they spotted the decoy, they started bobbing their heads and working closer in a circling fashion. Finally, the does were nose-to-nose with the decoy.

— David Westmoreland

Finally, the does were nose-to-nose with the decoy and seemed convinced the fake deer was no threat. They began to feed right next to it. Now that I had three decoys instead of just one, how could a buck resist such temptation? After a short time, the does fed their way into an adjacent field, but I was encouraged because the decoy had attracted the does and not scared them.

About an hour later I was watching a group of gobblers in the field when I heard a swishing sound behind me. I turned to see an 8-point buck doing that sideways walk toward my decoy. His hair was standing on end and his ears were laid so far back you could hardly tell he had any. About every third step, the buck would cut loose with a snort-wheeze to challenge my decoy. The buck came all the way into the decoy and, after no response and a close inspection, he began feeding near the decoy. The buck hung around 10 minutes and then wandered into some nearby timber. Right then, I was hooked on decoying deer.

Since that day I've used deer decoys many times and the results have always been pretty much the same. I've not had any deer spook from my decoy, and every buck that has seen the decoy approached. Some come on the run, others, like that first buck, come in looking to do battle. One thing is for sure, using a decoy really adds excitement to the hunt.

Westmoreland's Tips

✓ I've noticed that every buck approaching the decoy constantly licks his nose, evidently trying to gather scent to get a read on the decoy. That's why it's important to keep the decoy free of human scent.

✓ When I started using a decoy, I would just leave it in position overnight if I knew I was going to hunt the same stand the next morning. Then one morning I found my decoy had been smashed to pieces during the night by a buck.

John L. Sloan

As he does on most subjects, John Sloan, an outdoor writer from Tennessee, uses a unique approach to share his perspective on decoying.

John Sloan of Tennessee might be snake-bitten. Even though he has used decoys on several occasions, he's never had much luck with them. It just goes to prove that no matter how much success some folks have with a hunting method, not everyone will experience the same excellent results.

Some Guys Have all the Luck

Across the Alberta prairie a mere 350 yards away, stood one of the biggest bucks I've ever seen. I crouched lower into my haystack blind and watched through the binoculars as he swiveled his head, tasted the wind and stared at my decoys.

He started my way, pausing every few steps to check on things and survey the open barley field. "Come on," I silently urged him. Just another 335 yards and I'll have the shot. He kept coming, stopping just 300 yards shy of my bow range. But hey, that was better than most of the results I've had with decoys.

The day after the monster buck refused to come into my decoy, I sat in the same haystack and watched a forkhorn buck tear my decoy to shreds. I sat and watched as my decoy was hooked, pawed and then freshened with the world's purest deer urine. Because this little buck is the only deer I've ever had come to a decoy, I now wish I had shot him, just so I could say I've killed a deer over a decoy.

While hunting in Iowa one year, I had the perfect setup for a decoy: a

Using two decoys at the same time can add realism to your setup, and make deer less cautious about approaching.

gas-line cut between two thickets. All of a sudden I heard a commotion in the thicket and the sound of animals running my way. I got a good rest and flicked off the safety on my muzzleloader just as they burst out of the thicket.

The first animal was a collie. The second was a mix of some sort. Dogs three and four appeared to be offspring of one and two. All four tore into my decoy.

Someday I'll kill a deer over a decoy.

Ernie Calandrelli

Ernie Calandrelli, who works for the Quaker Boy game-call company in New York state, gets around when it comes to hunting whitetails. Wherever Calandrelli travels, you can bet a decoy goes with him.

Short Hunt, Wary Buck

Having just arrived in Ohio, I only had one hour to set up a stand and hunt the first evening. I really didn't think I had a prayer of arrowing a good buck, but I was anxious to be hunting. I put my decoy about 15 steps out into a cut cornfield and ran my climber up a nearby tree. I was just barely up the tree when a deer stepped into the corner of the field.

I picked up my binoculars for a quick look and nearly had heart fail-

Ernie Calandrelli has killed some big bucks over a decoy, but he says he has just as much fun watching the antics of bucks as they knock down or fall in love with "that hunk of plastic."

While I fumbled around trying to find my grunt call, the buck stopped to make a scrape and work the overhanging branch. Finding my grunt call, I grunted once and the buck immediately jerked his head up.

— Ernie Calandrelli

ure. The buck was about a 150-inch 10-pointer, and I didn't even have an arrow nocked. The buck jumped the fence and began walking down the fence line away from me. From where he was, he couldn't see the decoy.

While I fumbled around trying to find my grunt call, the buck stopped to make a scrape and work the overhanging branch. Finding my grunt call, I grunted once and the buck immediately jerked his head up and looked my way. I grabbed the line I had attached to the tail of my decoy and gave it a jerk while grunting once more. That did it. Mud flew from his hoofs as the buck ran toward the decoy and circled downwind. I realized that in my haste to get into the stand, I had not placed the decoy far enough downwind. The buck was now only 12 steps away from my tree, but he was head on and I did not have a shot. I was at full draw, but decided not to risk the frontal shot. Then he hit my scent. With a snort, the buck wheeled and ran across the field. I learned my lesson that evening. Even if pressed for time, take a few extra minutes to make sure the setup is right.

I've been fortunate to kill some nice bucks over the decoy, but I think I've had just as much fun watching the antics of smaller bucks fall in love with that hunk of plastic. I've seen them run in and knock my decoy down, and many times I've had their racks hang up in my tail line. The decoy is a real pain to carry sometimes, but the benefits are worth it.

Calandrelli's Tips

✓ I add a real deer tail to my decoy and then tie fishing line from a Zebco 202 spin-cast reel midway up the tail. By tying the tail in the middle, I can easily twitch the tail when a buck hangs up out of bow range. This tail twitch is all it takes to convince them the decoy is real.

✓ I like to use a decoy when hunting big clearings or field edges, someplace where deer can see the decoy from a distance. Get their attention with a grunt call and then let the decoy do its work.

Greg Miller

If I had not written this book, Wisconsin's Greg Miller would have. Miller has decoyed as many mature bucks as any hunter I know. Here, in his words, are some of Miller's favorite decoy memory:

A Memorable Lesson

I've witnessed many encounters between big bucks and decoys since about 1994, but one experience stands out most in my mind. Surprisingly, the experience did not result in a dead buck, either. It did, however, provide two crucial pieces of information about decoying. One, it proved to me that decoying could effectively lure bucks into bow range. Two, it proved that even a mature buck can be duped by a decoy.

The place was western Iowa in 1995. Late in the afternoon of Nov. 5, a monster buck strolled into a CRP field. He was about 500 yards from my stand. I grabbed the antlers and started rattling as loud as I could. The buck heard the commotion, looked my way,

Greg Miller

spotted the buck decoy in front of my stand, and started eating up the yardage in that easy lope big deer use when they want to get somewhere in a hurry. After several tense minutes, the 14-point brute finally decided to close in on my decoy. Unfortunately, I erred in estimating the distance of the shot. I used my 20-yard sight pin on a deer that was more like 30 yards away. My arrow skimmed just under the chest of this world-class whitetail.

My experience with the big buck taught me another valuable lesson. I learned not to give up too quickly on my decoy setups. The next morning I returned to the same stand from which I had missed the 14-pointer. Shortly after daylight, my rattling antlers caught the attention of another big buck. Unlike the events of the previous day, however, this time things turned in my favor. The 130-class 10-pointer that approached my decoy hesitated too long. His mounted head now adorns my trophy room wall.

Miller's Tips

✓ Make sure your decoy is odor-free. I scrub mine down with odor-killing soap and then leave it outside to dry. Each time I handle my decoy I spray it down with an odor-killing spray.

✓ Always place your decoy upwind of your stand site. I place my decoy between 15 and 25 yards from my stand.

✓ I always use scent with my decoy. If using a buck decoy, I'll use pure buck urine or tarsal gland scent. If using a doe decoy I will use a doe urine or estrous urine.

✓ To realize a high response rate, I use decoys where they can easily be seen. Alfalfa fields or picked corn or soybean fields are ideal in farm country. In big-woods settings, look for clearcuts, grassy swamps or logging roads.

✓ Don't place your decoy in the same spot every time out. This is especially important if a buck has seen the decoy but failed to respond. Changing the appearance of the setup even a little can work wonders the next time around.

Curt Wells
Curt Wells calls North Dakota home, but often slips across the river into Minnesota to decoy white-tailed deer.

Butting the Doe
The rut was on and I was doing the all-day thing, sitting in my stand from dawn to dusk. About 10 a.m., I heard the unmistakable sound of deer hoofs in dry leaves. God, I love that sound! It was a decent buck, about 115 inches B&C, but less than my desires for that time of the season.

The rut was going full bore and the buck was the fourth I had seen that morning. At the same time I spotted the buck, he saw my decoy. I happened to set up my decoy as a doe that morning. Because the buck was alone, I figured I had made a good gender choice, but things didn't work out that way.

After a few moments of eyeballing the decoy, the buck slowly approached it. But instead of circling to the rear of the decoy as bucks normally do when approaching a doe decoy, this buck headed for the front of the plastic temptress.

Because I had decided to pass on the buck, I reached for my camera instead of the bow. I had just gotten focused on the decoy when the buck walked into the viewfinder, headed for a face-to-face encounter with the decoy. I didn't know what to expect, so I pushed lightly on the shutter release. The buck stuck his nose out, touched the decoy's nose and jerked his head back like a turtle pulling its head into its shell. In a blur he lowered his head and rammed the decoy in the chest. By the time he realized some-

> *After a few moments of eyeballing the decoy, the buck slowly approached it. But instead of circling to the rear of the decoy as bucks normally do when approaching a doe decoy, this buck headed for the front of the plastic temptress.*
> — Curt Wells

thing was wrong, he had stumbled over the decoy's body, which scared him to his core. He got to his feet, bolted about 50 feet and then turned to look at the decoy. For five minutes the buck stared at the fallen decoy. Finally he wandered off, stiff-legged and confused.

I have no idea why the buck reacted that way. That is the first and only time I've witnessed such behavior. By the way, 10 days later, after the gun season began and I had lower expectations, the same buck wandered too close one more time. I punched his one-way ticket to my freezer.

Tom Kunz

I know plenty of good hunters who are not outdoor writers or TV personalities. Take Tom Kunz of Minnesota, for instance. When not hunting, he makes his living selling boats and RVs. But each November, you'll find Kunz hunting big whitetails over his favorite decoy. And he's good at it too!

Caught Flat-Footed

I had been on stand a couple of hours that October afternoon. It was getting close to 4 o'clock, time for another rattling session. I like to rattle about every 30 minutes while on stand. On this hunt I was using a doe decoy set up on a ridge edge with a steep drop just past and about 25 yards upwind from my stand in a big oak tree.

I gave a couple of grunts as I usually do before starting a rattling sequence, waited a few minutes and then started grinding the antlers together. I had only been rattling about 30 seconds when I spotted a buck coming at a dead run. I didn't have time to drop the antlers and grab my bow. The buck skidded to a stop eight yards away and looked at me. I thought his eyeballs would pop right out of his head.

As the buck stared, I felt the wind switch slightly. A breeze blowing from the decoy to the buck brought him the smell of the deer scent I had put on the decoy. The buck jerked his head around and spotted the decoy. He looked at me, looked at the decoy, flicked his tail and turned to walk to the decoy. When he ducked behind a tree, I exchanged antlers for my bow and nocked an arrow. I would never have been able to accomplish that if not for the buck's attention being focused on that decoy.

The buck walked toward the decoy but stopped 10 yards short of it. Because he was facing directly away from me, I had no shot. All I could do was wait. Twice the deer looked back at me, as if to make sure I had not moved. I could tell he was getting nervous and ready to make his move. When he did, I was ready. The buck grunted once and turned to leave. When his right leg moved forward and he turned broadside, I released and watched the arrow find its mark. The buck ran 25 yards, stopped, turned to look back at the decoy and went down.

Kunz's Best Buck

Here is the story of how Kunz got his best buck, a bruiser of a Montana buck that made it into the B&C record book. Even though it does not involve a decoy, rattling and calling were major factors.

Muzzleloading Monster

Two of my favorite times to hunt whitetails is when it's snowing or raining. Deer can be very active then, and I can move slowly and still-hunt effectively. Still-hunting is my favorite way to hunt deer, especially when the rut is on and I can rattle and call in conjunction with still-hunting.

This November day was perfect. The wind was coming down the mountain right into my face, and a fresh skiff of snow made for quiet footing. I found a lot of sign in the fresh snow where bucks had been chasing does during the night, plus numerous fresh scrapes. It was one of those days when you just know something good will happen.

I had made three sets, calling and rattling as I worked my way to a big flat about one-quarter of the way up the mountain. Nothing had responded, but I was not discouraged. I knew that the flat itself represented my best chance for bringing in a buck. By the time I reached it, rain began to fall, but there was still enough snow that I could easily see the flat was littered with buck sign. I found a spot for another rattling session, leaned my muzzleloader against a tree, and started with a series of grunts, as I usually do. A buck answered with a grunt from about 150 yards above my position.

Some hunters claim you can't hear a buck grunt that far away, but in the wilderness, where there are no noises from farms or highways, you can hear a buck grunt from a considerable distance. The wind was in my favor, so I sat and waited a couple of minutes to see what would develop.

The buck grunted again, but this time he was much closer. Then I could hear him walking down the mountain. The buck stopped behind a screen of brush. For two minutes I waited, but he did not budge, so I risked one more grunt. That did it, the buck came at a steady walk, grunting with every step.

At about 100 yards he stopped and stared right at me. I know he was looking for the buck he had heard, but it looked as though he were staring holes right through me. I had the sights on him and my finger on the trigger, but I remember coaching myself to just wait. I was sure the buck would walk in and give me a 30-yard shot. In my excitement, however, I must have put just a tad too much pressure on the trigger. I've heard it said that a good rifle shot is always surprised when his rifle goes off.

Well, I was sure surprised when that muzzleloader went off!

I could not see through all of

Tom Kunz of Minnesota could write a book filled with stories of his most memorable decoy hunts for whitetails. Kunz also spends much of his hunting time calling and rattling as he still-hunts for whitetails.

the smoke, but I heard the unmistakable sound of a hard running deer, and the sound was coming right at me. At 15 yards, I saw the buck charging down the hill on a collision course with me. He spotted me at the same time, dodged to his right and went barreling past me and down the mountain. I wanted to throw the gun at him!

I looked for some sign of a hit as he sped past me, but I could not see any and assumed I had missed. I was digging for a quick-loader when I heard the buck crash. I ran to the spot and found him. He was a magnificent animal in the prime of his life. I felt grateful and humbled.

CHAPTER 18

Putting it All Together

C alling, rattling and decoying can all stand on their own as viable tactics to pull more deer within shooting range. But when you use two or even all three of these techniques in conjunction, you maximize results.

When I first discussed the idea for this book with Patrick Durkin, the editor of *Deer & Deer Hunting*, my plan was to do a book on decoying only. I knew from my seminars and from talking with a lot of deer hunters, that there was growing interest in decoying deer. I also knew that good, solid, no-nonsense, comprehensive information on the topic was scarce. Durkin was genuinely excited by the idea, but suggested that rather than devote an entire book to decoying, that I work in some information on calling, rattling and decoying. "After all," he said, "they complement each other."

Reading back through what I've written, I know Durkin's idea to include sections on calling and rattling was the right decision. In fact, to have concentrated on decoying tactics without first covering calling and rattling in depth would have been a disservice to the book's readers. Certainly, there are plenty of times when deer are attracted to a decoy without the stimulation of rattling or calling, but in most cases, calling comes into play when decoying deer.

An Exciting Combination

Allow me to share an example of how I put all three of these tactics to work for the most exciting day I've ever had in the deer woods. Here's what I had to say about that day in my hunter's log:

"Nov. 5, 1997. Buffalo County, Wis. Heavy overcast and spitting snow early. Clearing and a high in the 20s with a light NW breeze later in the morning. After the warm weather we've had the past few days, this day is perfect.

"I'm hunting at Tom Indrebo's place. The bucks are really scraping up a storm right now and starting to chase every doe they see. I put my decoy out in front of my tree stand in the southwest corner of a large, ridgetop, harvested cornfield. It was one of those days when everything just felt right. The weather was good and the rut was on. I had good vibes.

"And what a day it turned out to be. I saw seven different bucks, six of which came into the decoy and did their thing. Man, what a show! The only drawback was that none of the bucks were the caliber I'm holding out for. But I don't really care. It was a day I'll never forget. Can't wait until morning!"

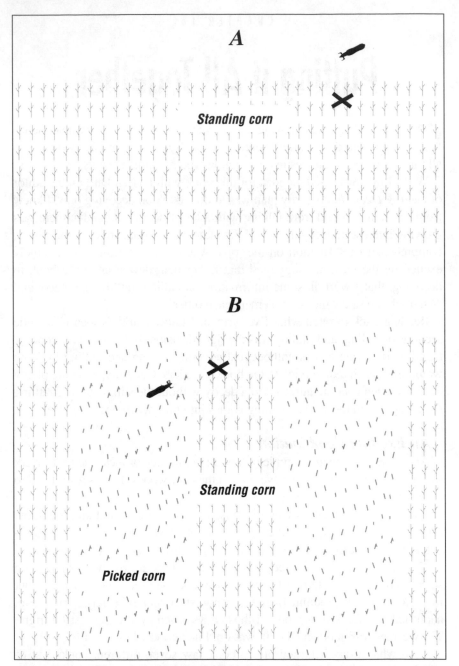

STANDING CORN SET: Deer use standing corn for feeding and bedding. As the season progresses and less standing corn is available, decoys become more effective when they're A) placed on the edge of standing corn, and, better yet, B) placed in a harvested strip in a partially picked field.

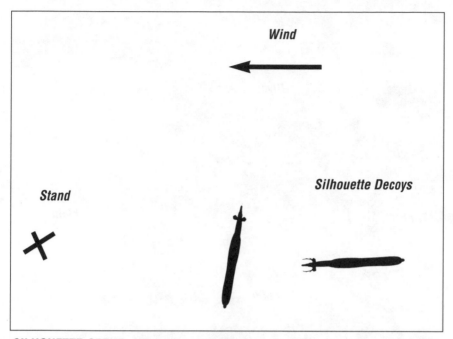

Wind

Silhouette Decoys

Stand

SILHOUETTE SETUP: When the author uses silhouette decoys, he normally uses two of them and positions them as shown here. This allows deer to see at least one of the decoys from all directions. This helps keep the decoys from "disappearing" when a deer approaches the setup.

How did I come into such excitement in one day? That morning — as I do most mornings during peak time for rattling, calling and decoying — I did not waste much time getting started. Bucks are most active in the morning, and I try to capitalize on that trait by using every minute of it to my best advantage. As soon as it was light enough to see my bow's sight pins, I gave a series of tending grunts. I then waited a few minutes and went to work on the horns.

Quick Reaction Time

I had just hung up the rattling antlers when I heard a deer coming from behind me. The buck came in from straight downwind but never smelled me. A lot of people laugh at how fussy I am about odor control, but it pays off many times each season. By the looks of the buck, I would say he was 3½ years old. He had a perfect 5-point rack on the left side, with good tine length and "wrap-your-fist-around-this" mass common to mature Midwestern bucks. Unfortunately, the main beam on the right side was snapped off above the brow. Maybe he had been in a fight, or had a close call with a car bumper.

Maybe he had a chip on his shoulder because of his half-rack, but this buck

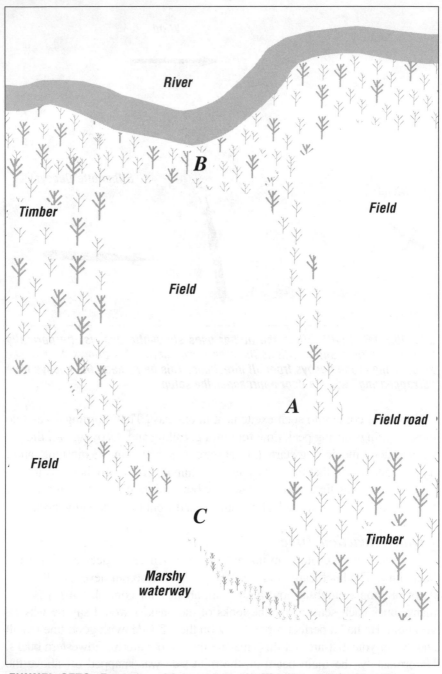

FUNNEL SETS: *Funnels, either man-made like the one in Location A, or natural, like the ones at locations B and C, are ideally suited for deer hunting over decoys.*

> *When a buck is covering ground trying to find the scent of a hot doe, he typically puts his nose low to the ground and just starts walking. Such possessed bucks will often go nonstop for hundreds of yards.*

had an attitude problem. I was sure he was going to take the decoy out. He walked in all jaunty and stiff-legged, as bucks do when they're putting on a show. The hair atop his neck was bristling, which made his already swollen neck appear even larger. His ears were laid back flat, and when he sidled up alongside the decoy I could see the whites of his eyes. It was quite a show.

I think he would have charged the decoy within the next few seconds, but just then a doe with a small buck on her heels came blasting out of the timber about 200 yards down the field. They made a heck of racket running across those dry, frozen cornstalks. The big half-rack heard them, turned, took one more look at the decoy, and then ran off in hot pursuit of the doe.

That buck was not gone 10 minutes when I heard another deer walking in the frozen leaves behind my stand. From the steady, unbroken cadence of its steps, I figured it was a buck out cruising. When a buck is covering ground trying to find the scent of a hot doe, it typically puts its nose low to the ground and just starts walking. Such possessed bucks will often go nonstop for hundreds of yards.

I gave a series of tending grunts with a couple of doe bleats mixed in. The buck liked what he heard. I first spotted him 75 yards back in the timber when he crested the ridge. One look through the binoculars and I knew he wasn't the buck I was looking for. He never hesitated as he approached. He just walked right past my stand and into the cornfield. With three points on his left beam and two on his right, the buck was obviously a 1½-year-old deer. When he spotted the decoy, he just stood and stared at it for maybe 15 seconds, and then turned and walked away down the field edge. I maybe could have grunted him back in if I had wanted, but I let him get on with his day.

Next Up, an 8-Pointer!

The little 5-pointer was barely out of sight when I saw another buck come out of the woods on the same trail the doe and her small buck had used earlier. It looked like this buck was trying to follow the doe's track, but was having trouble staying with it. It was fun to watch him weave back and forth across the corn stubble like a drunken fraternity brother. I tried getting his attention with the grunt call, but he was 200 yards away and the wind was blowing

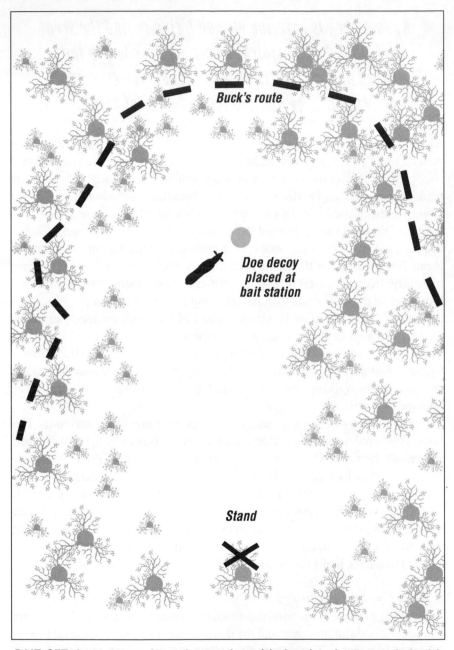

BAIT SET: *In states and provinces where it's legal to hunt over bait, it's common for bucks to cruise back in the brush and check on bait sites without ever actually coming to the bait. These bucks look and smell for does at the bait. If they don't see or smell a doe, they keep cruising. Placing a decoy or two at the bait site might coax such bucks into the open.*

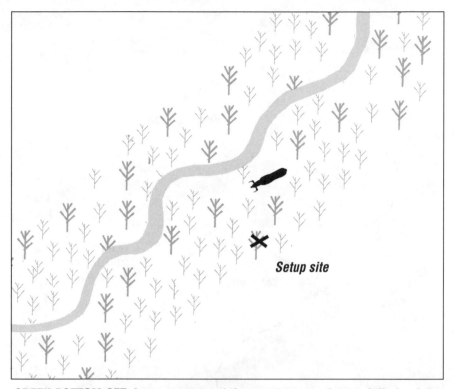

Setup site

CREEK-BOTTOM SET: In many parts of the country — and especially in plains states like Kansas, Nebraska, Oklahoma, the Dakotas and eastern Colorado, Wyoming and Montana — skinny creek bottoms provide most or all of the wooded cover for whitetails. These narrow, tree-studded creek bottoms are perfectly suited for using decoys.

from him to me. I'm pretty sure he never heard the call.

He sure heard the rattling horns, though. When I meshed the tines together and shook them, he threw up his head, stared my way a moment, and then hot-footed his way across the field. I don't know if he saw the decoy at first or not. He had an 8-point rack, but it was spindly and inside the ears. He came around and touched his nose to the decoy's nose. Oh man, I wished he was the buck I had been looking for, because he was posed perfectly for a shot. He hung around for a few minutes and then wandered off.

I couldn't believe it. I had seen four bucks in less than an hour, and three of them had offered good shooting opportunities. I didn't see another deer until 9:45 a.m. That's when another young buck, another 8-point basket rack, came all the way across the cornfield to the decoy. As he paraded around the decoy, I looked around to make sure no other deer were watching. I then practiced

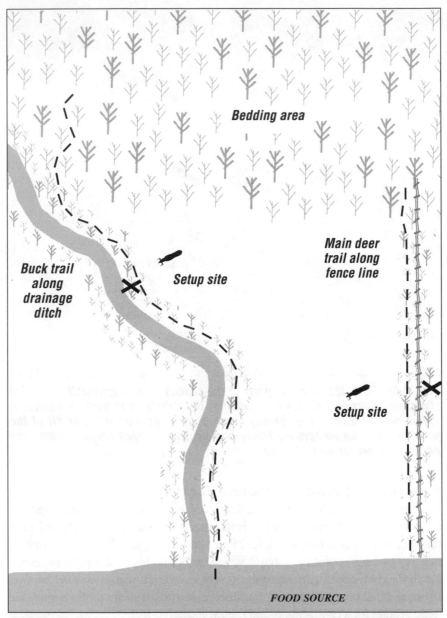

Bedding area

Main deer
trail along
fence line

Buck trail
along
drainage
ditch

Setup site

Setup site

FOOD SOURCE

PARALLEL TRAILS: One of Myles Keller's favorite places to hunt bucks is along a parallel trail. Keller says it's fairly common for big bucks to travel the same direction as other deer and move between the same general areas as other deer, but they seldom use the same trails used by other deer. The big boys usually use a parallel runway. In such cases as the scenario above, make your setup along the buck's parallel trail or along the main trail within sight of the parallel trail.

When I meshed the tines together and shook them, he threw up his head, stared my way a moment, and then hot-footed his way across the field. I don't know if he saw the decoy at first or not.

drawing on the buck. Three or four times during the minute or two the buck hung around, I drew on him. He never knew a hunter was within miles. Try that without a decoy!

At just a few minutes after 11 a.m., I had just finished another rattling session when I heard a buck running up the hill through the timber behind my stand. I was expecting a real bruiser looking to kick some butt. Instead, a spike buck ran right under my tree, blasted into the cornfield a couple of yards from the decoy, took one look at the decoy, spun and headed right back where he had come from. I don't know what the little guy expected to find!

Is This One a Shooter?

It was nearly 2 p.m. when I saw what ended up being the last buck I saw that day. I had gone through another series of tending grunts, followed by a minute-long rattling session, and had waited nearly 10 minutes without seeing anything. I was going to give the horns another exercise session when I saw a buck approaching from the far end of a field that was maybe one-third mile in length. He came on fast right along the edge of the timber. I took one look through the binoculars, picked up my bow and got ready. This one looked like a shooter.

I thought he was going to barrel right on in, but he slowed to a walk about 70 yards out and went into that stiff-legged, ears-laid-back, ain't-I-bad mode. The buck's mouth was hanging open and he was breathing hard. I don't know how far away he had been when he heard the horns, but it must have been quite a piece.

He was not the biggest buck I had seen that fall, but he was good enough for me. He was a basic 10-pointer with one broken brow tine and what looked like a sticker or maybe a fork on his left G-3. I really didn't look at the rack too closely. I just knew my heart was pounding and blood was rushing through my temples. Any deer that can do that to me will make my book, and that's the only book that really counts.

I was already calculating the shot. I knew the buck would circle around to the front of the decoy, because mature bucks nearly always approach a buck decoy from the front. When he did, I knew he would offer a perfect broadside

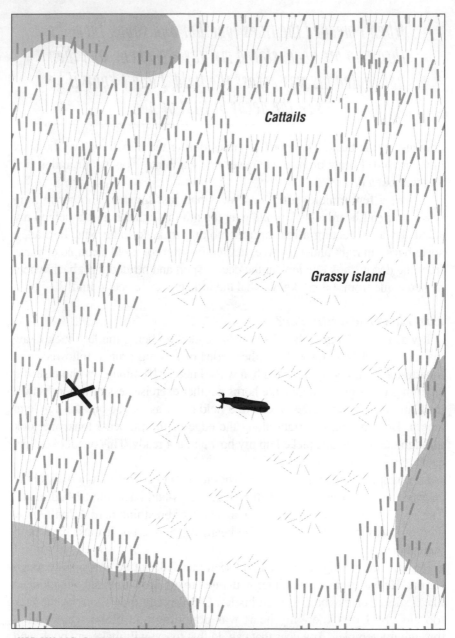

JIM HILL'S SWAMP SET: *Jim Hill of Minnesota is a master at hunting the marshes. Big cattail swamps harbor big bucks, because the swamps are so nasty few hunters venture into them. After all, how do you hunt a buck in a couple-thousand acres of cattails? Jim Hill has learned to seek out grass islands in the cattails, and use a decoy to bring in bucks that patrol these grass islands for hot does.*

When it comes to using decoys for whitetails, today's hunter has a wide variety to choose from. Shown above are some of the many commercially manufactured models available.

Decoy Manufacturers

Manufacturer	Addresses	Phone Number
Carry-Lite	5203 W. Clinton Ave. Milwaukee, WI 53223	414-355-3520
Come-Alive Decoy Products	4916 Seton Place Greendale, WI 53129	414-421-2840
Custom Robotic Wildlife Inc.	839 Oak Road Mosinee, WI 54455	715-692-3000
Feather Flex/ Outland Sports	8675 W. 96th St., Suite 204 Overland Park, KS 66210	913-341-7350
Flambeau Products	Box 97 Middlefield, OH 44062	440-632-1631
Higdon Motion Decoys Inc.	7 Universal Way Metropolis, IL 62960	618-524-3385
Mel Dutton Decoys	Box 113 Faith, SD 57626	605-967-2031
Montana Critter Co.	4405 Buttercup Lane Missoula, MT 59802	406-728-8196
Montana Decoys	Box 2377 Colstrip, MT 59323	406-748-3092
Outlaw Decoys	624 N. Fancher Road Spokane, WA 99212	509-927-2750

shot. And because his attention would be riveted on the decoy, I knew I could get away with drawing and shooting, even though I didn't have much cover in the leafless green ash in which I perched.

The buck was now 30 yards away and circling in from my right to left. My feet were in position, my release was on the string, and my emotions were under control. Everything was perfect.

Hee-Haw Time

And then the damned mule showed up! I heard it coming. The buck heard it, too, and stopped to stare back in the woods where the steady crunching of heavy hoof grew louder and louder before a big, black mule with a brown face topped the ridge. Riding the mule was a man in a red and black checkered wool coat.

The buck, evidently as amazed as I was, stood his ground for maybe 30 seconds. I thought for a moment I might get lucky. Maybe the mule and rider would pass and the buck would still come into the decoy. But when the rider reined the mule to a halt, the buck turned and went slinking away so quietly that even though the guy on the mule was only 30 yards behind my stand, he never heard or saw the buck. A minute later the mule and the rider were gone.

I learned later that the guy was a timber cruiser. He used the mule, which was trained to jump fences, to get around in the rugged coulee country. Unfortunately, the timber cruiser spent the rest of the day riding in the area I was hunting, marking trees suitable for harvest. If I had known he was going to spend that much time nearby, I would have gone somewhere else to hunt the rest of the afternoon. Who knows how many more bucks I might have seen that day if that mule had not shown up.

Even though I never dropped the string, I consider that November day to be the best time I've ever had hunting with a decoy.

How many of those bucks would I have seen and been able to shoot if I had used only a grunt call, or only rattling antlers or only a decoy? I don't know. This was not research conducted under controlled conditions in which I could duplicate everything and compare results. This was a real hunt.

So Many Bucks

No matter. I believe that calling, rattling and decoying — all working together and complementing each other — led to all the action I experienced that day, and so many other days before and since.

What if I had just climbed up into my stand and sat there? No calling, no rattling, no decoy. How many of those bucks would I have seen? How many would have offered me good shooting opportunities?

Again, there's no way to know, but my guess is maybe one, if I was lucky.

I do know one thing. I would have missed out on a ton of fun!

About the Author

This is Gary Clancy's third book on hunting white-tailed deer, a pursuit to which he freely admits a hopeless addiction. The only relief is more hunting. Clancy hunts whitetails in at least a half-dozen states and provinces each season.

Clancy is a versatile hunter, hunting whitetails with bow and arrow, muzzleloader, centerfire rifles, shotguns and handguns. When not scouting, watching or hunting deer, Clancy is usually writing about deer hunting. He has written hundreds of magazine articles on all aspects of white-tailed deer hunting.

He lives in Byron, Minn., with his wife, Nancy, and daughters Michelle, Kelli Jo and Katie.

Whitetails by the Moon
by Charles J. Alsheimer, edited by Patrick Durkin
Charles J. Alsheimer, Deer & Deer Hunting magazineπs Northern field editor, explains how deer hunters can use autumn moon cycles to predict peak times in the North and South to hunt rutting white-tailed bucks. He details the ground-breaking research conducted that unlocked the mysteries of the moonπs influence on deer activity and behavior.

Softcover • 6 x 9 • 256 pages
100 b&w photos
LUNAR • $19.95

Rub-Line Secrets
by Greg Miller, edited by Patrick Durkin
In Rub-Line Secrets, Greg Miller takes deer hunters to the graduate level in teaching them proven tactics for finding, analyzing and hunting a big buckπs rub-line. No one has enjoyed more rub-line success than Miller. His straight-forward approach to hunting rub-lines is based on more than 30 years of intense hunting and scouting. The book is illus-trated with photos and diagrams that help Miller explain his proven rub-line tactics.

Softcover • 6 x 9 • 208 pages
100 b&w photos
HURU • $19.95

Bowhunters' Digest
4th Edition
edited by Kevin Michalowski
This fully updated edition will help you find active deer, choos a perfect stand location and put your broadhead right where counts. You know nothing tops the thrill of setting your sight pin behind the shoulder of a monster buck. Now, some of America's hottest hunters share their tips to help you achieve the bowhunting success you've always dreamed of.

Softcover • 8-1/2 x 11 • 256 pages
300 b&w photos
BOW4 • $19.95

Satisfaction Guarantee: If for any reason you are not completely satisfied with your purchase, simply return it within 14 days and receive a full refund, less shipping.

Shipping & Handling: $3.25 1st book; $2 ea. add'l. Call for UPS delivery rat Foreign orders $15 per shipment plus $5.95 per book.
Sales tax: CA 7.25%, VA 4.5%, IA 6%, PA 6%, TN 8.25%, WA 8.2%, WI 5.5%, IL 6.25%